PROPERTY OF
MYRON I. SIMMONS

RECEIVED 7-2-83

BOOK NO. 753

SHEPHERDS & SHEEP

A Biblical View of Leading & Following

Jerram Barrs

Foreword by Howard A. Snyder

InterVarsity Press
Downers Grove
Illinois 60515

© Jerram Barrs 1983

Published in England under the title Freedom and Discipline. *Published in the United States of America by InterVarsity Press, Downers Grove, Illinois, with permission from Universities and Colleges Christian Fellowship, Leicester, England.*

All rights reserved. No part of this book may be reproduced in any form without written permission from InterVarsity Press, Downers Grove, Illinois.

InterVarsity Press is the book-publishing division of Inter-Varsity Christian Fellowship, a student movement active on campus at hundreds of universities, colleges and schools of nursing. For information about local and regional activities, write IVCF, 233 Langdon St., Madison, WI 53703.

Distributed in Canada through InterVarsity Press, 860 Denison St., Unit 3, Markham, Ontario L3R 4H1, Canada.

All Scripture quotations, unless otherwise noted, are taken from the Holy Bible: New International Version, copyright © 1978 by the New York International Bible Society. Used by permission of Zondervan Bible Publishers.

Cover photograph: Shostal Associates, Inc.

ISBN 0-87784-395-3

Printed in the United States of America

Library of Congress Cataloging in Publication Data

Barrs, Jerram.
     Shepherds and sheep.

    Includes bibliographical references.
    1. Christian leadership.   2. Authority (Religion)
I. Title.
BV652.1.B37   1983   262'.8   83-314
ISBN 0-87784-395-3

18	17	16	15	14	13	12	11	10	9	8	7	6	5	4	3	2	1
97	96	95	94	93	92	91	90	89	88	87	86	85	84	83			

FOREWORD

Renewal is often painful. We resist growth, and we grow painfully. But this is part of the cost of embracing the Spirit's renewing work in the church today.

Leadership and authority quickly emerge as problems in times of renewal, because every group requires leaders. We soon learn that the impelling force of the Spirit does not cancel out the need for decisions, human authority and recognized leaders. And here is the rub: The new leaders—regardless of how sensitive, intelligent or spiritually mature—are still human and therefore fallible. And no way of grouping fallible leaders together ever makes them infallible! The church must seek its direction and authority, not primarily in leadership structures, but in the authority of Scripture interpreted by the collective sensitivity and maturity of the *whole* body of Christ —the whole Christian universal priesthood—guided by the Holy Spirit.

Jerram Barrs's book is useful precisely at this point. The author rightly recognizes that the issue at stake in current abuses of shepherding and eldership is the New Testament doctrine of the priesthood of believers. The need for authority in a renewal group can quickly push it into repeating the errors of the past—particularly in creating a new special priesthood which, with undoubted sincerity and spiritual-sounding justification, soon takes upon itself more authority than God intends. But it is the *whole church*, according to Scripture, which is a kingdom of priests.

I find this book most timely and useful. I am in sympathy with all those today who are rediscovering the meaning of the church as community, the gifts of the Spirit, and plural leadership or eldership in the church. But I believe the emphasis some groups put on hierarchical leadership structures, "covering" and the so-called "chain of command" is a distortion of New Testament principles which needs attention and correction. The author of this book takes a balanced, biblical approach which can help the church find a healthier understanding of leadership and shepherding.

I do not agree with the author at one or two points. In particular, I am not convinced that in the New Testament apostleship is confined to the original eleven plus Paul; it seems clear to me from the New Testament witness that even in Paul's day Barnabas, James and others were considered to be apostles. I do agree, however, with the point the author wants to make here: We are not to recognize the teaching of any leaders today as on the same level of authority as the apostolic teaching in the New Testament. One of the greatest dangers in any movement is the tendency to give the teachings of its leader or leaders the same weight as Scripture. This, in fact, is one thing that distinguishes a cult from a genuinely Christian church. Any group, regardless of how spiritually alive, runs the risk of veering off from biblical orthodoxy when it gives too much weight to the decisions of a small group of leaders, forgetting those leaders' own humanity and vulnerability.

The point is that the Bible does not offer us any structure of leadership in the church which guarantees protection against the fallibility of our leaders. In my view, hierarchical or "chain of command" structures are particularly dangerous because they have no biblical basis and may so easily be abused by sincere Christians with the best of intentions.

This book is a useful biblical critique of leadership patterns that should help both older churches and newer Christian communities to think through the issues in shepherding and to find the kinds of patterns which will make for spiritual health and vitality. Biblically, all believers are gifted priests and ministers. I commend this book as a timely and practical reminder of that fact.

Howard A. Snyder

INTRODUCTION

"We are so fortunate. Our minister does so much for us. Besides preaching and taking the service twice on Sundays, he gives a Bible study on Wednesdays, goes to the old people's home to take a little service each week and visits everyone who is sick. He takes so many details about church matters on his own shoulders. Isn't it a blessing he is such a willing worker? Though I have wondered lately—seeing him looking so strained—whether we ought to see if we can help him in some way."

☐ "When the congregation didn't give him the necessary two-thirds majority, the minister called another meeting two weeks later to vote again. This time the motion was passed, but it caused some bad feeling, I can tell you. He had gone round and got all kinds of people who were still on the membership roll to come and vote for what he wanted. Some of them hadn't been to church for years, and I think some of them don't even claim to be Christians now. It made me feel that the congregation was just a rubber stamp that had been faulty the first time round."

☐ "A church needs commitment. Members must agree to come to weekly fellowship meetings on Tuesdays as well as the worship on Sundays. If you are unable to keep this commitment one week, we expect you to let one of the elders or your group leader know. Also, if you are facing any important decision for yourself or your family, please come and talk to us about it. We feel it is good for everyone to submit decisions to the elders for prayer and counsel before going ahead."

☐ "Don and Jennifer, we want to talk to you about your children. The elders feel, after watching them for some time, that they are not properly disciplined, especially Henry, your nine-year-old. What we plan to do is to place Henry in an elder's family for two or three years. He could have a weekend with you once a month."

☐ "Only last month Richard left his wife and moved in with Cathy, the choir director. Everyone knew he had been seeing her for several months, but this is going too far. I know this is supposed to be an enlightened age and we are not to be judgmental, but shouldn't the church say *something*?"

☐ "Thus says the Lord: 'It is wrong to take out insurance of any kind.' To have insurance means you are not trusting God for your daily bread. You are all to cash in your insurance policies. There are many needs in the church for which the money could be used in a spiritual way."

These examples are drawn from different church traditions. Each tells us something about the pattern of ministry followed in its church, and the extent of its commitment to authority. Some churches are run by the firm ministry of one person; some have seen that power abused. Some churches monitor every aspect of their people's lives, while others by default condone gross immorality. You may applaud some as examples of good shepherding, or you may have grave doubts about such "thorough" shepherding.

All the examples above point either to the problem of structure or to the question of freedom. How can we have church structures which will help people? How can we avoid structures which will be so rigid that they inhibit growth to maturity?

1
IRON FIST OR MORAL CHAOS?

We all want the freedom to live our own lives and make our own choices, the genuine freedom that creates a garden of life and beauty. But freedom sometimes leads to license, where individuals do what is right in their own eyes, hurting others and hurting themselves, creating a wasteland where life is destroyed and ugliness reigns. How can we affirm genuine freedom but avoid its abuse?

This is an important practical question to ask. Both in society in general and in the church in particular there is a tension between freedom and authority. How much freedom should the individual Christian exercise, and how much authority should be given to leaders? What structures should govern the life of the church?

The world today illustrates the problem clearly. In some countries there is excessive authority. Governments, without the people's consent, impose brutal structures and laws. There is no freedom to question, to protest, to vote against the powers that be. Such crushing and oppressive use of authority leads not to life but to death.

In the West, on the other hand, we have freedom—freedom to question, to protest, to vote against the government. But this freedom has for some become license; the liberty which should lead to life has become instead a basis for selfish and sinful desires to rule our choices. The apostle Paul saw this danger and warned us: "You, my brothers, were called to be free. But do not use your freedom to indulge the sinful nature; rather, serve one another in love" (Gal 5:13). We can see only too clearly in our culture what a wasteland such indulgence brings about. Sexual license has made marriage and family life an empty desert for many people. Selfishness and greed on the sides of both laborers and leaders have produced the same effect in many work places.

Are these alternatives, rigid structure on the one hand and license on the other, the only options? Is it inevitable that we in the church duplicate this scenario and err in one direction or the other? Too often we as Christians simply recycle the problems and tensions of our culture. Instead of heeding the apostle's warning "Do not conform any longer to the pattern of this world, but be transformed by the renewing of your mind" (Rom 12:2), we allow ourselves to become copies in miniature of the society in which we live. Before examining a biblical answer to the questions about freedom and authority, let us look briefly at some of the problems in our churches.

(1) **Believe What You Like**

The problem of license exists in the church just as it does in our culture. License is freedom which knows no bounds, which refuses to submit to any structures, freedom gone wild. Its only constraints are "I think" and "I want."

In society at large the divorce rate is leveling off significantly. Among professing Christians the divorce rate is still increasing rapidly. In thinking about this and other ways that the church is copying the selfish freedom of our culture, I am reminded of a friend's atheist professor who predicted several years ago that by the early 1980s evangelicals would be the most worldly group in the church.

In contrast, Scripture offers us freedom within the framework of what is true. "You will know the truth, and the truth will set you free" (Jn 8:32). The Bible sets down clearly the basic teaching which Christians should believe. It gives a plain account of the righteousness and love which ought to characterize our lives. It vividly describes what kind of caring and mutually edifying community a living church should build. Yet, sadly, when non-Christians look at the church, they may find no clear guidelines for what they should believe, how they should live or what a church should be.

Too often churches, like our society, have become permissive. There has been a doctrinal permissiveness. Scripture speaks simply and directly about who God is and who we are; about creation, sin, judgment and salvation; about Jesus' historical death, resurrection and coming again. It speaks so simply that a little child can understand. Yet these clear doctrines have been subjected to twisting, reinterpretation, avoidance, and even open rejection and scorn by some theologians and ministers—without any fear of discipline. An extreme example is *The Myth of God Incarnate,* a book which denies the deity of Christ and even suggests that to call Jesus "God" is blasphemous.

Even some evangelical ministers and theologians have been influenced by the skepticism of critical theories. Some have redefined the authority of Scripture, thrown out angels and devils, watered down the nature of judgment and questioned the historical accuracy of large parts of the Old Testament. Believers are left in confusion, wondering what they can believe in Scripture, wondering where they can turn for instruction in sound doctrine and refutation of those who oppose it.

(2) Do As You Please

The church has become at times morally permissive, just as society at large. Where Scripture speaks straight about moral issues, the church sometimes equivocates. Although Scripture, for example, teaches that homosexual practice is wrong and calls the homosexual offender to repentance and to faith in the forgiveness of Christ, some churches discuss whether to ordain practicing homosexuals and recognize homosexual "marriage." Although Scripture forbids the taking of innocent life, some churches and theologians advocate abortion on demand and infanticide. Again no one has been disciplined over such issues. *The Guardian* ran an article about a large, flourishing church. The reporter asked the church's representative about its stand on various moral issues, such as divorce, homosexuality and abortion. The representative replied, "We don't take stands on controversial issues." The reporter commented, "This is Christianity without commitment, faith without repentance."

We are called to be the salt of the earth, a city set on a hill, a light shining in the darkness of our culture (Mt 5:13-16). Jesus calls us to teach and be examples of righteousness before our society. But are we? When unbelievers look at us, do they see a distinctive righteousness in marriage and family life, in business integrity, in hard and honest work, in concern for the poor and needy, in visiting the widow and orphan, in the pursuit of justice for the unborn, the handicapped and the elderly? When people look at us, how often do they see our good deeds and praise our Father in heaven? How many of our churches practice the discipline for unrighteousness that is commanded by God's Word: discipline for immorality, greed, idolatry, slander, drunkenness, swindling and idleness (1 Cor 5:9-11; 2 Thess 3:6)?

This lack of moral distinctiveness makes genuine community in the church almost impossible. Our society emphasizes self-fulfillment so much that the seventies were called the "me" decade. We are encouraged to think of our own needs, desires and rights, and not to worry about the needs of others. Often the evangelical church's emphasis on personal salvation and sanctification, though good in itself, leads to the impression that the church is there purely for *our* benefit. We are tempted to a kind of pious selfishness. Do our churches challenge such attitudes? Not much.

But God's Word does. Paul calls us to value others more highly than we do ourselves; Jesus commands us to serve one another (Phil 2:3; Jn 13:14-15). When we do, the church becomes a community of believers who genuinely care for each other, who share in each other's joys and sorrows as well as grieve with each other's sins, who support each other practically and financially, who care for the needy within the fellowship and beyond it.

As a negative example, I know of a young woman with two children who was deserted by her husband and subsequently divorced. In time she became a Christian and joined a widely respected church. But in two years as a member no family ever invited her and her children into their home, despite her hardship in being a single parent and despite James's word that the "religion that God our Father accepts as pure and faultless is this: to look after orphans and widows in their distress" (Jas 1:27). Now that one-parent families make up more than fifteen per cent of all families, this need presents a tremendous challenge to our churches.

Perhaps the grossest example of license in our culture is materialism, the headlong pursuit of money and possessions. *Things* are our culture's idol, mammon the god before whom so many people bow and to which they dedicate themselves. Shopping has become the pastime which distracts them from boredom, from thought and from facing the emptiness of their lives.

Are we different as Christians? We quite rightly stress that God has created all things good, to be enjoyed and received with thanksgiving (1 Tim 4:4; 6:17), and we point out that material prosperity may be a sign of God's blessing. But this grateful receptivity can subtly come to mirror our culture's materialism. Scripture does speak of blessing for obedience (Deut 28 and 30; Mt 6:33; Eph 6:2-3), but we cannot excuse an indolent, luxurious lifestyle on the grounds of God's blessing. Jesus warns us against trying to be "both/and" Christians, lovers *both* of God *and* of money and possessions: "You cannot serve both God and Money" (Mt 6:24).

(3) **Purity—Appearance or Reality?**
Not all churches, of course, have been permissive about standards of behavior and faith. The desire for purity has, in fact, precipitated discipline for doctrinal unfaithfulness, and for that we should be thankful. But sometimes a concern for pur-

ity can degenerate into a separatist spirit, a mentality which is applied to smaller and less important areas of disagreement. This is an ugly mentality, and it does much damage.

A more widespread problem, however, is that of legalism, the establishment of a rigid set of evangelical dos and don'ts. On the one hand are the don'ts: you must not drink, smoke, dance, go to movies, play cards. Legalists argue that Christians should not do these kinds of things because their witness would be damaged by such worldly activities. On the other hand are the dos: you must wear particular kinds of dress, attend certain meetings, give the outward appearance of spirituality.

The problem here is that we can become genuinely confused about our spirituality; we may feel that because we are fulfilling these regulations we are truly spiritual. This, however, is the very mistake the Pharisees made. It is far too easy for us to become hypocrites and feel that because we look spiritual outwardly, because we are Christians publicly, therefore all is well with our lives. We need to remember Jesus' admonition to his disciples, "Be careful not to do your 'acts of righteousness' before men," and his judgment of the Pharisees, "Everything they do is done for men to see" (Mt 6:1; 23:5).

The Problem with Rules

All human rules have built-in problems. First, and most insidious, is that we can think we are obeying God and being really spiritual when in fact we are simply obeying human rules. The rules may actually stand as a barrier between us and God in that they prevent us from seeing the poverty of our spiritual condition.

God's commandments, "You must rid yourselves of all such things as these: anger, rage, malice, slander," "Love the Lord

your God with all your heart and with all your soul and with all
your strength and with all your mind," and "Love your neighbor as yourself" (Col 3:8; Lk 10:27), strike at the heart and
expose our sinfulness. We have to acknowledge that we are
unprofitable servants. Human rules which apply only to the
outside are so much easier to keep! But keeping human rules
may engender pride: "I am avoiding worldly things," when, in
fact, I may not even have begun to sort out my life in matters
of *real* worldliness—boasting, the lust of the eyes, envy, selfish
ambition, greed, impurity, sexual immorality (1 Jn 2:15-16;
Jas 3:14-16; Col 3:5).

   Second, human rules can too easily become absolutes for
our lives. We all need some rules, some structures for orderly
family or church life. However, we must never make the mistake of thinking or implying that these are of the same order
as God's law. His commandments are absolute and unchang-
ing. They must not be relaxed. "Anyone who breaks one of
the least of these commandments and teaches others to do the
same will be called least in the kingdom of heaven" (Mt 5:19).
In contrast, human rules are only adopted for certain practical reasons. They must therefore always be flexible so that
they may be abandoned at a moment's notice if they hinder
life rather than help it.

   These criticisms must be applied even to the rules we make
about prayer, Bible study and evangelism, activities which are
perfectly good in themselves. We are on dangerous ground
when we make rules about these matters, rules which have to
be observed for Christian living and spiritual growth. The
motivation for imposing such rules may be good: to help people to grow in their understanding of Scripture, in their
prayer life and in their evangelism. However, the rules themselves may create bondage and actually inhibit people from

having the freedom to read Scripture, pray and share the gospel.

Why is this? Regardless of motive, to impose forms which Scripture does not lay down and to insist that they be obeyed, that they be a measure of spirituality as well as *the* means of growth, can easily create a bondage mentality. It paves the way for either pride—I do it and therefore I feel spiritual—or despondency—I do not do it and therefore I feel guilty. Sometimes Christians become spiritually crippled, finding prayer and Bible reading difficult and frustrating, because they have been pressured into obeying certain rules. They are made to feel guilty. And then they find it more and more difficult to keep the rules, and guilt feelings increase even further.

God himself has not given these rules. They cannot be found in the New Testament. What we find in the New Testament are commands to grow in our understanding of the truth, to pray without ceasing, to bring all of our requests to God, and always to be prepared to give an explanation for our hope (2 Tim 3:14-17; 2 Pet 1:12-15; Rom 15:14; 1 Thess 5:17; Phil 4:6; 1 Pet 3:15). But we do not find rules about how to do these things. Christians are free to work out for themselves what is most helpful as they read Scripture, bring their requests to God and share the gospel with others. The church reminds new believers of scriptural commands and should provide examples among its members of these commands lived out in practice. But the Holy Spirit leads each individual to his own unique pattern—a pattern of prayer, Bible study and evangelism that fits his unique personality.

In some churches the iron fist of tradition may be invoked to strangle any kind of new life. "We have always done things this way," it is said, even if the reason for the practice in question disappeared a hundred years ago. Formulas, endlessly

repeated, lose their meaning. Ironically, again, this can be at
its most stifling in a "free" context where the services are not
set. The issue here is not liturgy itself but the presence or
absence of Spirit and truth in worship.

Sometimes tradition is more subtle in its power over church
members. It may be taught openly or implied by attitude that
everybody has to have the same experiences. Again a bondage
mentality develops. The individual feels, "I have to be like
them; my inward experience of Christ has to be just like
theirs." Such conformism can crush people, creating in them
a sense of spiritual alienation and homelessness so different
from that sense of belonging which God desires for his children. Some are tempted, perhaps subconsciously, to *pretend*
to have experiences which others have had. This is regret-
tably common.

Longing for Reality

Conformism, legalism, lack of commitment and spiritual un-
reality: these are problems the church faces today, problems
that frustrate and estrange many believers.

Many churches have responded by striving to realize
greater purity of personal life and Christlike caring in their
community through faithful teaching. Christians turn hun-
grily to such churches, for they see the doctrinal laxity in
their own church and long for a living commitment to the
Word of God. They see moral permissiveness and long for
heartfelt obedience to the commands of Christ. They see lack
of community and caring and long for a fuller experience of
the body of Christ, where all share each other's burdens and re-
joice and suffer together. They see legalism and long for freedom in Christ. They see conformism and long for the enjoyment of diversity which the Spirit desires the church to have.

A new problem, however, arises: What structure shall be created to ensure the development of commitment and community? In trying to find a structure which will create life in a church, we are dealing with the issue of form and freedom. Because so many evangelical churches evidence little shepherding of the flock and little application of biblical discipline, those searching for a new way have often erred in the direction of creating forms which are too rigid. These may inhibit an individual's growth in dependence on the Spirit and may limit unnecessarily his or her freedom in Christ. The reaction against looseness and materialism may give rise to too much authority.

Are we bound to live always at the extremes, in both society and church, either with structures that inhibit individual maturity or with a liberty which leads to license, where commitment and love are lost? Is there an inevitable tension between form and freedom? Looking at our society and the church, we might be tempted to answer yes. Can we ever find structures that do not impinge too far on personal liberty, but which make life possible? Can we find freedom that is not license, but life giving?

Fortunately the answer to these latter questions is yes, and the resolution lies in the relationship between the Word of God and the work of the Holy Spirit. It is to this relationship between Word and Spirit that we now turn in the next chapter.

2

THE WORD AND THE SPIRIT

*H*ow does the internal work of the Holy Spirit relate to the written Word of God, the Bible? Many Christians are guilty of setting one against the other almost as if they were mutually exclusive. One group has the Word; another group has the Spirit.

Those who have "the Word only," neglecting the Spirit, tend to be legalistic and tradition-bound. They read Scripture through the spectacles of their forbears and are blinded against any fresh and living insight into Scripture's teaching. Their churches need the fresh wind of the Spirit to blow away the dust of the past and to help them wake up to the twentieth century; they may find that their church has become a ghetto, isolated from the culture in which they live. Their problem is not that they have the Word but that they may be reluctant to let the Spirit teach them what the Word actually says.

Those who "have the Spirit" may become so excited by their newly found liberty that they neglect the written Word, feeling they have a "hot line to heaven." Paul writes, "Now the Lord is the Spirit, and where the Spirit of the Lord is, there is freedom" (2 Cor 3:17); some have misunderstood this freedom to mean freedom from the written Word. For example, Witness Lee of the Local Church Movement, referring to Romans 7:6 ("we should serve in newness of spirit, and not in the oldness of the letter" KJV), writes that the letter from which we are released is the written Bible.[1] He thus sets up a conflict between the written Word of God and the internal work of the Holy Spirit.

A Hot Line to Heaven

This example is extreme, but unfortunately there is in some evangelicalism a tradition that harbors suspicion of doctrine, suspicion of using one's mind to understand Scripture and suspicion of law or any human effort to obey the law of God. This tradition suggests that when we have the freedom of the Spirit, we do not have to pay attention to the written commands; we need not obey them. A recent booklet states, "The Law no longer regularizes and directs our life from without, but is a life-giving principle within, which both inspires and enables all thought and action."[2] It has, in effect, set up tension between the law of God written in Scripture and the law of God which the Holy Spirit is writing in our hearts.

Thank God there *is* a life-giving principle within us through the power of the Holy Spirit! But should we therefore have less regard for commandments written in Scripture? The same writer says that "the Spirit creates inner righteousness," which is certainly true, but he then goes on to say, "There is no written or external law in the new covenant." Or again, "the commands and instructions of the New Testament, for example, the Sermon on the Mount, are not given to become a new code of behaviour for us to obey. We do not obey the commands as such, we obey the voice of the Spirit in our heart."[3] Here again the author sets the written Word against the inner activity of the Spirit.

We find the same tension in Watchman Nee. Application of the mind to Scripture is discouraged because the mind is a part of "the self," "the soul," "the outer man," and gives only natural understanding. But the Holy Spirit speaks directly to the intuition, "the spirit," "the inner man," and this gives spiritual understanding.[4] Nee has the same problem with application of the will to obey God's law, as the will is also seen as part of the soul; only obedience which flows without effort from the spirit is seen as acceptable to God.[5]

This neglect of the mind, the will and the written commandments of God leads to problems. The stress on intuition and spiritual understanding, the hot-line-to-heaven mentality, leads to genuine confusion for some young Christians as to how to discern the will of God. How can they be sure that what they think is the voice of the Spirit speaking in the "inner man" is not in fact their own natural self?

We ought not be surprised when we find that precisely these writers and churches, which have stressed their newly found liberty of the Spirit and have a suspicion of law and commandments, have had to create new structures to help people find God's will. Sometimes these structures have become authoritarian. In fact, one can predict that the greater the de-emphasis on Scripture, the mind and the law, the more authoritarian the structures will be. For example, people who have been involved in the Local Church testify, on the one hand, to a tremendous emphasis on the liberty of the Spirit and a neglect of the Word (because the Word is said to *bind* people. On the other hand, they describe the oppressive authority of a leader who tells everybody what to do, who so totally controls everyone's life that some members live in fear of making any independent decisions.

The central question here is this: Should such a contrast be made between the Spirit's work and obedience to the written commandments?

The New Testament knows nothing of such an opposition between the Spirit and the Word. It rejects the legalism of the Pharisees and the Judaizers. It rejects the legalism which demands that gentile believers obey those parts of the Mosaic law which applied distinctively to Israel.[6] It rejects legalism which insists we earn salvation by works of the law. The New Testament rejects also any legalism which subjects people to human traditions rather than to Christ:

> Since you died with Christ to the basic principles of this world, why, as though you still belonged to it, do you submit to its rules: "Do not handle! Do not taste! Do not touch!"? These are all destined to perish with use, because they are based on human commands and teachings. Such regulations indeed have an appearance of wisdom, with their self-imposed worship, their false humility and their harsh treatment of the body, but they lack any value in restraining sensual indulgence. (Col 2:20-23)

This passage does not mean, however, that law itself has no place for the believer, who is redeemed by the work of Christ. Paul insists rather that "the law is spiritual": "I am not free from God's law but am under Christ's law" (Rom 7:14; 1 Cor 9:21).

Be Filled

The New Testament has, in fact, as positive an attitude to the Word and the law as it has to the Spirit. Paul writes,

> Do not get drunk on wine, which leads to debauchery. Instead, be filled with the Spirit. Speak to one another with psalms, hymns and spiritual songs. Sing and make music in your heart to the Lord, always giving thanks to God the Father for everything, in the name of our Lord Jesus Christ. (Eph 5:18-20)

Compare the Ephesians passage with Colossians 3:16-17:

> Let the word of Christ dwell in you richly as you teach and admonish one another with all wisdom, and as you sing psalms, hymns and spiritual songs with gratitude in your hearts to God. And whatever you do, whether in word or deed, do it all in the name of the Lord Jesus, giving thanks to God the Father through him.

Paul then goes on to speak about submission and service in the family, in the home and at work, just as he does also in Ephesians.

Notice how remarkably similar these two passages are. The only substantial difference between them is that the one opens with the admonition "Be filled with the Spirit," and the other with the call to "let the word of Christ dwell in you richly." One commands us to meditate on and fill our hearts with the Word of Christ, the Holy Scripture, God's law; the other commands us to be filled with the Spirit. The implication from these parallel passages is that the two commands express similar thoughts. The Word of Christ, the Scripture, is to be central in our lives if we desire to please the Spirit, to be filled with the Spirit.

In chapter five we will examine carefully the view that "the Word of the Lord" is the gift of prophecy rather than the objective Christian message once and for all given through Christ and his apostles. For now I will assume the conclusion of that discussion, so that we should understand that Paul is calling believers to "let there be ample scope for the proclamation of the Christian message and the impartation of Christian teaching in their meetings. Christian teaching must be based on the teaching of Jesus Himself; it must be unmistakably 'the word of Christ.' And it would 'dwell richly' in their midst when they came together and in their hearts as individuals if they paid heed to what they heard, bowed to its authority, assimilated its lessons and translated them into daily living."[7] We are to have all our thoughts, words and deeds controlled by and centered on the Word of Christ found in Scripture itself.

Other passages also speak to the importance of not separating the ministry of the living Spirit from the written Word. "From the beginning God chose you to be saved through the sanctifying work of the Spirit and through belief in the truth" (2 Thess 2:13). Compare this with Jesus' statement in his high priestly prayer for his people: "Sanctify them by the truth; your word is truth" (Jn 17:17). The one passage tells us that sanctification comes by the Spirit, the other that it comes through the Word. Jesus says to Nicodemus, "Flesh gives birth to flesh, but the Spirit gives birth to spirit. You should not be surprised at my saying, 'You must be born again' " (Jn 3:6-7). Compare this with 1 Peter 1:23: "For you have been born again, not of perishable seed, but of imperishable, through the living and enduring word of God." We are born again by the Spirit, and we are born again by the Word.

Jesus ties the Spirit and the Word together when he says that the ministry of the Spirit will include the giving of the Word: "The Holy Spirit, whom the Father will send in my

name, will teach you all things and will remind you of everything I have said to you" (Jn 14:26; see also Jn 16:12-15). And
Paul, writing about the whole armor of God in Ephesians 6,
says, "Take . . . the sword of the Spirit, which is the word of
God" (v. 17). Calvin comments on this relationship between
Word and Spirit: "As soon as the Spirit is separated from the
Word of Christ, the door is opened to all kinds of delusions
and impostures. . . . The written doctrine appeared to them to
be literal and therefore they chose to contrive a new theology
that would consist of revelations."[8]

The New Testament teaches us that the Word of God is the
weapon that the Spirit uses to direct both the church and the
individual believer. To depend on the written Word is not
to neglect the Spirit, but rather to use the weapon the Spirit
has given for our defense and teaching.

Be Free

We see in the following two excerpts a most instructive com-
parison.

Where the Spirit of the Lord is, there is freedom. (2 Cor
3:17)

Do not merely listen to the word, and so deceive yourselves. Do what it says. Anyone who listens to the word but
does not do what it says is like a man who looks at his face
in a mirror and, after looking at himself, goes away and
immediately forgets what he looks like. But the man who
looks intently into *the perfect law that gives freedom,* and continues to do this, not forgetting what he has heard, but
doing it—he will be blessed in what he does. (Jas 1:22-25)

On the one hand, Paul says it is the Spirit that gives liberty.
On the other hand, James says it is obedience to the law of
God which gives liberty.

There is no tension in the New Testament between Word and Spirit, between law and freedom; rather the two work in harmony. Why is this? Why can Scripture interchange the terms *Word* and *Spirit,* the attributes of the Word and the Spirit, and the effects of the work of the Word and the Spirit?

The simple answer is that the Spirit himself is the author of the Word and has given his commandments there for our instruction. Therefore, if we want the Spirit's liberty, any church structures we create must be subject to the guidelines the Spirit has laid down in the written Word. The new wine of the Spirit can be contained only in the Spirit's own wineskins.

Behind this simple answer lies a very profound issue, an issue which involves our understanding, first, of God's knowledge and goodness and, second, of the positive nature of his law; these stand in stark contrast, respectively, to our human finiteness and sinfulness and to the problematic nature of human laws and structures.

Our Limitations

God is our Creator. He is the infinite God, but we are finite, created creatures. Because we are finite, all we can ever have is a limited perspective on reality and on our lives. We can never know enough to know all the answers, to erect a system of thought that will answer our every question. This is why every human religion and philosophy is always doomed to be inadequate; it begins from a finite person trying to create a system of thought big enough to answer every question. No human can ever do this, simply because we are finite. Even if we could put together all the wisdom of all the human beings who have ever lived, it would still be finite. We could never find or create a big enough answer.

If we consider the problem of morals, how we should live, the same difficulty arises. As humans we are unable to generate from ourselves and from our experiences laws, moral commandments and forms that can always and everywhere be absolute. Neither an individual looking into his own heart or at his own experience, nor a society as a whole, is able to tell us finally what is right and wrong.

A society may, however, *pronounce* what is right, and it can do so in more than one way. In a dictatorship, the few who have power tell everybody else what to do: might is right. Freedom for the many is lost in the arbitrary law rigidly imposed by the few. Or, as in the West today, the majority may rule. That is, the state pronounces as right whatever the majority of the society thinks is right: fifty-one per cent is right. But in point of fact, the fifty-one per cent may not be right.

Consider our changing laws—the abortion law or the laws on homosexuality. A few years ago our laws said one thing, that abortion and homosexual acts were wrong. Now the consensus has changed, and under certain circumstances abortion and homosexual practices have become "right." What was wrong yesterday can be right today. What is right today may be wrong tomorrow, and vice versa. We need to understand that this changeableness is inevitable because as finite persons we are too little to make laws, structures or forms for human life which will be always and everywhere adequate. As finite persons we tend to err either on the side of license—being too lax, too permissive—or on the side of being too rigid, too legalistic.

This is why it is such a problem when we add new laws to the Word of God. Whenever new rules are added and everybody is expected to obey them in addition to the Word of God, the consequence is legalism, which degenerates into Pharisaism. We can never create forms that will be always and everywhere right. We are finite.

The confusion is increased because we are sinners as well: we really do not know what is right because we desire in our fallen human hearts to do what is wrong. The self-centeredness and deceitfulness of the human heart tend to make our finest human aspirations and longings come out twisted. "The heart is deceitful above all things and beyond cure. Who can understand it?" (Jer 17:9; see also Rom 7:15).

So we must test all structures we create for our churches against the Word of God. Otherwise we may find that either we will lose the liberty the Spirit intends or we will allow practices God's Word forbids. Either we will endorse too much authority or we will encourage license. In one church no one will be disciplined even for immorality; in another someone will be disciplined for not attending enough meetings. In one church we shall become bogged down in questions of procedure endlessly and unnecessarily raised from the floor; in another we shall have no discussion at all—simply orders handed down from above.

God's Law

Must the individual, society or the church be condemned to this continual excess in one direction or the other? No, God has not abandoned humanity to its own devices. God is the Creator, the infinite Lord, the Alpha and Omega, who knows the end from the beginning, who inhabits eternity. Nothing is hidden from his eyes; there are no secrets before him; all knowledge is his. Because God is infinite, because his knowledge is complete rather than finite, he knows how we are to live, for he has made us to live in a certain way. God made us in his image to be like him and to reflect his character. His commandments point the way for us to live as his image bearers.

In Leviticus 19:1 Moses records a section of God's law: "Speak to the entire assembly of Israel and say to them: 'Be holy because I, the LORD your God, am holy.' " God has a particular character; we have been made in his image to have that same kind of character, to be holy like God himself. The commandments in Leviticus 19 express what God's character is like and what our character is to be like, as bearing his image. Verse 3 continues, "Each of you must respect his mother and father.... I am the LORD your God." "When you reap the harvest of your land, do not reap to the very edges of your field. ... Do not go over your vineyard a second time or pick up the grapes that have fallen. Leave them for the poor and the alien. I am the LORD your God" (vv. 9-10). Because God is faithful and compassionate to the needy, our character is to be so, too. That is the way God made us to be. "Keep all my decrees and all my laws and follow them" (v. 37). Why? Because "I am the LORD."

God is the one who is big enough to tell us what is right. So the law reflects God's holiness and prescribes what our lives ought to be like, as made to reflect his image. Jesus said that the Pharisees' yoke was heavy; they put burdens on people's shoulders which nobody could bear. But he went on to say, "My yoke is easy and my burden is light" (Mt 11:30). God's law is not restrictive; it is not a burden to us, and it will not crush our lives as human restrictions do. Rather it is directive. The law is God's Word given to show us how to live.

Because this is true, we may echo the exclamations in Psalms 1, 19 and 119, where the psalmist extols the commandments of God: "How I love your law! I meditate on it all day long" (Ps 119:97). The commandments of God are sweeter than honeycomb and finer than gold.

The Christian today ought to be able to say or sing these psalms with conviction and gladness because the law of God is given to us for our life and our liberty. Therefore James can write, "The man who looks intently into the perfect law that gives freedom, and continues to do this, not forgetting what he has heard, but doing it—he will be blessed in what he does" (Jas 1:25). And thus Paul can say the Word of God is the sword of the Spirit (Eph 6:17). If we want forms which will give us life, we are to listen to God's Word. We are to read God's Word and see what he says we should do.

This truth is something we should delight in, for it is profound in its implications. In any area of human life—in our individual lives, in our marriages, in our families, in the society as a whole, in the church—as we obey God's commandments and conform to the structures he has given, we have liberty. Form and freedom are not opposed to each other if the form we adopt is the form that God has given. Any church structure we adopt or authority we impose in the church must be subject to the guidelines in Scripture. No matter how much we stress the liberty of the Spirit, we will lose it unless we humble ourselves before the Word.

3
SOME
DANGER
AREAS

I n the 1970s large numbers of evangelicals tried to find new structures which would enable the church to fulfill its calling before God. Of course, not *everyone* wanted new ways. Many Christians, especially young people, were frustrated when the elders of their assemblies blocked every new suggestion, however spiritual it was. Others complained that "in our church the clergy do everything and won't accept any changes."

But the desire for a fresh form of biblical community could not be crushed. In the face of the moral laxity and permissiveness in so much of the church, many Christians have longed for doctrinal and moral purity and biblical discipline, have longed for a restrained lifestyle in the church and for a community which cares for people in need. They have looked at the desert and said, "We want to create churches which will be springs of living water giving life to people, refreshing them."

With this motivation many churches have tried to develop forms of government which they hope will promote life. Some churches have used forms that already existed and simply increased the authority of the elders, ministers or pastors. Although this has been a move in the right direction, sometimes the authority has been applied to areas where Scripture does not require it. Other groups have tried to create completely new structures to contain the new wine of their commitment to a living church.

For those of you reading this who are involved in such churches, I appeal to you not to respond by simply taking offense at the questions raised and criticisms put forward in this chapter regarding the new structures. Rather, try to read them with an open mind, just as you read the criticisms made earlier about the lack of community and lack of genuine shepherding in much of the church. We will examine more of the biblical material on which these criticisms are based in chapters four, five and six, and I will propose there a positive alternative. For now, please bear with me. These criticisms are made in love; I appreciate the great need for churches to be lights in the enveloping gloom of our culture, cities set on hills so that they may be seen to be different, offering hope to the people and glory to God.

The Pyramid

Let us consider first those churches that implement firmer authority. Some have created a series of authority levels which rise from one step to the next, so that what is taught and practiced is a pyramidal form of church government. At the base of the pyramid is the flock, the people of God, the members of the church; next up the pyramid are the elders of the church, or shepherds; next in order are the bishops or district superintendents; higher still are the apostles; and at the top, of course, are Christ and the Holy Spirit. (In some churches there are no bishops—simply members, elders and apostles.) In this pyramidal form, authority ascends to the apostles, who themselves stand directly under Christ. It is insisted, of course, that the pyramid stands upside-down, as authority in the church means service; but there are nevertheless these rising levels of authority.

We may respond that this arrangement is not new. Many churches have been organized this way, with authority running from the people in the pew right up to the archbishop in his palace. But the traditional episcopal system does not necessarily involve the same kind of hierarchical form of government that some of the new churches have adopted. The traditional episcopal church guards the balance between the three houses of clergy, laity and bishops so that careful checks and balances limit all human authority. Traditionally, too, authority is circumscribed and defined by the doctrine and morals of Scripture.

The motivation for adopting such pyramidal forms of government has been thoroughly praiseworthy: to have order and not chaos; to get rid of society's permissive influence on marriage, the family and the church; and to encourage maturity through discipline. The aim is that the members of the church be made answerable to the elders, the elders answerable to the bishops and the bishops answerable to the apostles. Also, the authority exists in order to create commitment and community both by teaching and example. Sometimes this has meant that those in authority institute practical living structures which involve all the members of the church; the church may be divided into house units or communities with certain rules for their ordering.

Some churches and Christian communities have built their authority on an exalted view of the church. That is, they consider the church on earth to be Christ's presence, an extension of Christ's incarnation. With such a view it is easy for an authoritarian form of government to develop, for those at the head of the pyramid, the apostles, are seen as Christ's representatives on earth.

For example, the leaders of one such church write, "During the first three centuries the church held universally that the bishops or presbyters acted in Jesus' stead, and were invested with authority to found, establish and administer churches."[1] Quoting the early church fathers Ignatius and Polycarp, they argue that we ought therefore to regard bishops as we would the Lord himself, and that we should obey presbyters and deacons as God and Christ. The argument assumes that apostolic succession has continued to the present. Writes one, "We are of the Apostolic College. Our doctrine is pure and our practice is right, and we are doing what we are told."[2] (One must presume that, while other people are directed by men, the apostles are directed immediately by God.) The form adopted means that everyone must be in subjection to someone else. The question arises, What about the people at the top of the pyramid? To whom are the apostles subject? Their answer is that they are in subjection to each other and to the Lord.

No Accountability

To be fair to those who hold the office of apostle, I must say that most undertake the task with humility and a deep sense of responsibility. Many are genuinely subject to one another in a way which clearly demonstrates the presence of the Spirit of Christ. But, I would argue, this is in spite of the structure, not because of it.

If you give a group of people the name *apostles* and see these apostles as Christ's representatives on earth, and if one of them has a strong, dynamic personality, the end may sadly be the equivalent of a kind of pope—but one with far more control over individuals' lives than the Roman Catholic pope has ever held. Something like this developed among the "exclusive" Brethren; the leader had almost total control over people's lives. And, unfortunately, several new groups are moving in this same direction. So this is one problem: If there is a pyramidal form of government, an ascending view of authority without adequate checks and balances, everybody below becomes subject to those above, and those on top may have no person to whom they are accountable.

As I said earlier, the reason for adopting such a form is a good one, arising as it does from a desire for genuine leadership in the church. The New Testament clearly teaches government of the church by carefully selected and appointed leaders. "Paul and Barnabas appointed elders for them in each church and, with prayer and fasting, committed them to the Lord in whom they had put their trust" (Acts 14:23; see also 1 Tim 3:1-7; 5:17; Tit 1:5-9).

But what exactly does this government entail? How much authority should the elders have? What issues should be decided by the congregation as a whole and what by the elders alone?

It seems to me that two mistakes can be made. The first is for the elders to domineer over the congregation. In some churches every decision, whether for an individual, a family or a part of the church, has to receive the approval of the elders or "shepherds."

The second mistake is just the opposite, that is, for the elders to restrict themselves solely to pastoral work and teaching and provide no leadership, direction or government for the church. Immorality goes undisciplined. The church has no vision. The majority reigns: a two-thirds majority or a seventy-five per cent vote is needed to get even the slightest change in the church. The pervasiveness of this second scenario is precisely what has led to the development of new, often rigid forms of government.

If we want to encourage Christian growth in our churches, we would do well to imitate the flexibility we find in the New Testament. Consider some of the events recorded in the book of Acts.

Acts 6:1-6. A problem of unfair distribution of food gives cause for complaint. The apostles come to the congregation with a concrete proposal: Elect seven men to do the necessary work. This pleases everyone, and the congregation elects seven men.

Acts 10:24–11:18. Peter baptizes Gentiles and eats with them, marking a radical new direction for the church. He is criticized by fellow believers and explains to them the reasons for his decision, which of course affects the practical policy of the whole church toward Gentile believers. Everyone seems satisfied with his explanation (for the moment at least—problems do arise again later).

Acts 13:1-3. The leaders of the church in Antioch are led by the Holy Spirit to send Paul and Barnabas off to do missionary work.

Acts 15:1-34. The Jerusalem council meets to discuss what to do with Gentile believers, as some Jewish Christians are still demanding that they ought to obey the law of Moses and be circumcised. The council sends out its decision to all the churches. (This account is one of the reasons Presbyterian churches have presbyteries and synods of all the elders from the different congregations.)

In these passages we see both effective leadership and the desire to gain agreement. No one attempts to domineer over the congregation. Nor is any one way set down to direct how we should achieve such consensus.

It is wise to bring some issues, such as the election of elders or deacons, to a congregational vote, although the proposal to have elders or deacons may come from the leaders (Acts 6). Other matters, like discipline, are more appropriately handled on an individual level. New directions, such as sending out missionaries or church planters, may be decided by the elders (Acts 13), as may practical matters concerning the peace and growth of the whole church (Acts 10, 15). Elders may raise other issues for the discussion, prayer and decision making of the whole congregation.

Discussion and openness are needed both ways. The congregation must feel free to come to its leaders with ideas for direction, questions and even criticisms, as I will discuss later. Conversely, leaders must feel free to come to the congregation with ideas, proposals and decisions; that is, they must be *episkopoi,* or "overseers."

Can we indeed design a structure of authority which will avoid all problems, providing a clear way out of every difficulty which arises? The pyramidal view is an attempt to provide such an orderly solution, but the danger is that congregational consent may be lost. We may also become romantic about the possibility of perfection in church life.

Checks on Power

First, regarding agreement in the church, we should note that the apostles did not submit their decision to have seven deacons elected as a command. Rather the congregation was able to express its approval. Thus the NIV translates: "This proposal pleased the whole group" (Acts 6:5). The church then chose the individuals who would fill the office of deacon.

Second, regarding accountability, Peter was careful to explain his decision to eat with and to baptize Gentiles. He did not presume on his apostleship as if he were above question. He was prepared to explain his actions and to answer questions. He did not see this accountability as an assault on his authority (Acts 10, 11 and 15).

Third, with regard to perfection and the hope of finding a structure which will solve every problem of authority, we ought to take seriously the fact that the New Testament churches themselves experienced many problems concerning the exercise of authority. Problems arose between Peter and Paul in front of the whole congregation (Gal 2:11-14), between Paul and Barnabas over John Mark (Acts 15:36-40), and between Paul and the Corinthian church over several issues (2 Cor). These problems neither ended the fellowship nor caused despair that unity was not achieved instantly or, in the case of John Mark, for some considerable time. Rather Paul and Peter, Paul and Barnabas, and Paul and the Corinthians worked through these difficulties in time.

If they had problems, how much more shall we? So let us not give up—or assume that the solution lies in finding another structure by which we may avoid problems. Paul points the way forward:

Therefore, as God's chosen people, holy and dearly loved, clothe yourselves with compassion, kindness, humility, gentleness and patience. Bear with each other and forgive whatever grievances you may have against one another. Forgive as the Lord forgave you. And over all these virtues put on love, which binds them all together in perfect unity.

Let the peace of Christ rule in your hearts, since as members of one body you were called to peace. And be thankful. (Col 3:12-15)

Any structure we adopt must be circumscribed with love, forgiveness and forbearance, just as "love is the fulfillment of the law" in every other area of the Christian life (Rom 13:10).

Fourth, we need adequate checks and balances. What do I mean by this? A congregation must have the opportunity to ask questions, to agree to proposals and to criticize those in authority.

"But doesn't this undermine the elders' authority?" you may ask. "Isn't criticizing the elders equivalent to rebelling against God?"

According to Watchman Nee's understanding of the church, which we will examine in the next section, it would indeed be just that. But we must not make the mistake of equating human authority with God's authority. This same mistake is sometimes made in families, where a father feels that for him to acknowledge to his children errors in judgment or in discipline would undermine his authority, and that, because he is representing the fatherhood of God, he should never admit to mistakes in front of his children.

This is a serious misunderstanding. All of us are sinners—parents and children, elders and congregation. God is the only person who never has to apologize. As sinners saved by grace we all stand equal before him, needing to confess and needing forgiveness. We may be given different positions of responsibility and authority in the home and in the body of

Christ, but never does our position set us apart from our
fellow human beings. We must always therefore be ready for
our behavior and decisions to be questioned, discussed and
criticized. We must be open to correction and rebuke.

Scripture sets clear precedent for such openness. We saw in
Acts how Peter answered questions about his behavior with
Cornelius (Acts 11). Subsequently the apostles and elders met
to consider the issue once more, as there were still questions
and disagreement (Acts 15). Apollos, a teacher greatly used by
the Lord, was taken aside and instructed "more adequately"
in the truth by Priscilla and Aquila (Acts 18:24-26). Paul rebuked Peter publicly (Gal 2:11-14). Furthermore, Paul gives
some precise instruction about how to handle accusations
against elders: "Do not entertain an accusation against an
elder unless it is brought by two or three witnesses. Those who
sin are to be rebuked publicly, so that the others may take
warning" (1 Tim 5:19-20).

Such give-and-take among elders and between elders and
church people *is* possible in the church, by God's grace, and
will only enhance genuine authority rather than undermine
it. We are not to be like the world, lording it over one another
(Lk 22:24-27; 1 Pet 5:3), seeking status for ourselves (Lk
11:43; 20:46), afraid of losing face before others. Our confidence is in Christ, not in our authority; in Christ, not in the
pretense of always being right. Our authority is to be expressed in service, just as Jesus himself, at the very end of his
ministry, washed his disciples' feet (Jn 13). "Do nothing out
of selfish ambition or vain conceit, but in humility consider
others better than yourselves. Each of you should look not
only to your own interests, but also to the interests of others.
Your attitude should be the same as that of Christ Jesus"
(Phil 2:3-5). This model is for the Christian leader as well as

for the congregation. The humility of Christ is the leader's model.

Covering

Another problem which has come up is the teaching of the chain of command, or *covering*. Both in churches with a structure of members, elders and apostles and in churches with simply members and elders or ministers, some are advocating that every member must be in obedient submission to someone else; that is, each person must be "covered" by another. Many articles and books on the subject of shepherding and discipling teach precisely this.

Again, the motivation behind the idea of covering is a good one. People at the end of the twentieth century seem to have such fragile personalities. Christians so easily just copy the world when it comes to the priorities in their lives, particularly with regard to possessions and money and sexual and social behavior. Covering seems a good way to make sure that Christians do not make foolish and sinful decisions in these areas. But let us look in more detail at the ideas behind covering.

Covering is taught by the influential figure Watchman Nee; he seems to be a major source of the doctrine, as his books have been so widely read. Nee has a very high view of the church, a view which leads to a high view of authority in the church. He teaches that the church is one with Christ, but not just in the sense that the New Testament teaches, which is a oneness of relationship with Christ. For him it is much more than that: "What, in truth, is our understanding of oneness? Quite simply, oneness is God Himself. Why is this so? Because when all of us set aside the things outside of God and begin to live in Him, then God who is in us becomes the oneness."[3]

Such teaching blurs the distinction between the human creature and the divine Creator. The church in his view becomes the body of Christ in a literal way. It actually becomes the presence of Christ on the earth. Out of his view of the union of the church with Christ, Nee develops a correspondingly high view of authority: "We must not only submit as Christians to the direct authority of the head, that is Christ, but we need also submit to the indirect authority of the head [that is, church leaders]. . . . Consequently, whoever sees the body of Christ sees also the authority which God has set in the body of Christ for him to submit to and we must be submitted to it. . . . If you truly perceive the authority of the head you will also perceive that one or more members of the body are ahead of you and that to them you must learn to submit. Hence you recognize not only the head, Christ, but also those whom God has set in the body to represent the head. If you are at odds with them you will also be at odds with God."[4]

Nee teaches that whenever Christians disagree with their leaders, they ipso facto disagree with God. This teaching about authority has very practical consequences. "If a person does not know what authority is, how can he say he knows the body of Christ? That is to say that the one who knows the body can discern only when only three or five people are assembled together, who among those assembled is his authority, because there is manifested in their midst the authority of the head to which he needs to submit." What this means in practice is that wherever a few Christians meet together, even if only three or four, the group must recognize that there is someone among them to whom each one must submit, someone who is the group's authority. Nee continues, "When life and appointment agree, you must submit; otherwise, life will cease and you will be dislocated from the body thus signifying that you do not hold fast to the head."[5]

If Christians are not prepared to have this kind of submission to someone in authority, they will be separated from the body of Christ. Their lack of submission signifies that they do not hold fast to Christ, that their relationship to Christ is not genuine.

Nee makes it plain that he is referring not only to doctrinal and moral issues, where Scripture is clear, but also to the details and choices of an individual's life. He says in effect that if somebody who is in authority comes to you and tells you that they think you are doing something wrong, if you can see nothing in your life which is sinful, even after prayer and confession and carefully seeking the Lord's face, then you must be prepared to accept their authority over you. Even if the believer's own conscience knows no guilt, and even if examination finds nothing at all contrary to the Word of God, you must be prepared to submit, he says, "since Christ is in all of them, there He is in the midst of them. Where two or three are gathered in the name of Christ, the Lord will manifest Himself."[6]

This teaching suggests that the will of God cannot be known by the individual alone. Rather the mind of Christ can be known only in the context of a group and of submission to that group. "The apostles and the elders should be notified concerning any important affairs so that they may help you in unclear situations."[7]

Nee introduces the concept of covering when he discusses how a person can make decisions and discern God's will. No one should undertake alone to make decisions or face issues calling for discernment. He cautions that a believer who stands alone before God simply seeking God's will for his or her life is subject to Satan.[8]

Marriage and Home

The teaching of church involvement in personal matters, which has become quite widespread, reaches even into home life. It is taught that in marriage a wife is subject to Satan's attacks if her husband is absent, and therefore she must not make decisions alone; rather she and her decisions need always to be covered by her husband, by his authority. This is comparable to the teaching in the church that only when the believer stands *with* the body, *submitted* to its authority in all decisions, is he or she not subject to Satan. Nee emphasizes that the believer who stands by himself before the Lord is in spiritual danger: "Whoever is under the covering of the body of Christ is protected, for the body has this specific function: to serve as a protective covering. . . . The spiritual armor [of Ephesians 6] is given to the church and not to anyone individually." He warns, "Let me say that if you ever miss the body you will lose your covering and are thereby exposed to great danger."[9]

We must, of course, have a high view of the body of Christ. We must recognize that we all have been joined together in and for mutual interdependence as believers—to share our lives, to care for each other and to use our gifts to upbuild one another. And of course we need to be humble enough to ask advice of fellow Christians when we are perplexed. A prayerful group can be of great help and encouragement. But the New Testament does not teach that any decision, any issue in a believer's life, has to be covered by somebody else in the church, or else that person is in danger of attack from Satan. Nor does it teach covering in marriage, as if the wife were a spiritual inferior. "There is neither . . . male nor female, for you are all one in Christ Jesus" (Gal 3:28).

What does this teaching of covering mean in practice? It

demands that the individual believer's ideas, decisions, lifestyle, be covered by somebody else in the church—somebody else higher up the chain of command, higher up the pyramid. Should you get married? Consult your cover: your elders, ministers, fathers, pastors—whatever name is used for the authority in your church. Should your family move? Consult the cover. Whether you are considering a new job, pondering how many people should live in your home, how much money you should give or what you should buy, you must consult your cover.

This scenario is not a caricature or an exaggeration. A friend recently told me about a young couple who had been unable to conceive. We naturally suggested a specialist who had helped other friends in similar difficulty, but the wife responded, "I will have to ask the older woman who is covering me before I try to make an appointment." Countless people with decisions about marriage, financial expenditures, disciplining of children and home locations have chosen to be covered in this way.

What alternative does Scripture give us? What part can and should elders of a church take to encourage the reality of a caring community, and wise and sanctified personal decision making?

The first responsibility of elders is to be examples of godly living. They are not to be inaccessible preachers. Elders are called not primarily to deliver sermons to the congregation, but to practice hospitality and to be servants of the flock in practical ways: "The overseer must be above reproach" (1 Tim 3:2); "We were delighted to share with you not only the gospel of God but our lives as well" (1 Thess 2:8); "Be shepherds of God's flock . . . not lording it over those entrusted to you" (1 Pet 5:2-3). Jesus remained a foot-washing servant to the end of his earthly ministry. No leader ever moves beyond the call to be a servant of the flock.

Second, elders are responsible to teach biblical truth concerning those difficult areas of life where our culture so easily influences us. Materialism—the pursuit of money, possessions, comfort and luxury—is a serious problem among First World Christians. The New Testament urges us to teach about it. Hence Paul's word to Timothy: "Command those who are rich in this present world [almost all of us today in the West] not to be arrogant nor to put their hope in wealth, which is so uncertain, but to put their hope in God, who richly provides us with everything for our enjoyment. Command them to do good, to be rich in good deeds, and to be generous and willing to share" (1 Tim 6:17-18). We need clear teaching and "commanding" on these issues where obedience is so difficult. Paul, however, confines his teaching to the principles and the general commands in line with those principles. He does not spell out in a detailed program the precise choices that each individual must make. That has to be worked out by the individual before God.

Third, elders are responsible to counsel, encourage and rebuke on the personal level (2 Tim 4:2; Tit 2:15). The New Testament calls all believers to comfort, encourage and admonish one another (Gal 6:1-5; Col 3:16). This teaching, however, is not a mandate for making others' decisions for them. It means rather that we should be sympathetic and ready to listen, that we should be discerning enough to help others see the problems and dangers they must deal with. It means being sure of the Word in order to lay before fellow believers the principles and guidelines of behavior set out by Scripture, and being humble in order to communicate that we are fellow sinners redeemed by Christ and also in need of support. It means being spiritual in order to be able to point out faults and restore someone to godliness, and being dependent on the Lord so that we are always ready to pray with and for someone. It means believing so that we may encourage others to trust God for guidance and to seek wisdom from the Lord himself (Jas 1:5).

The Autocratic Pastor

Common in many churches, both those more traditional and those with new structures, is the phenomenon of one-man rule. A single pastor or minister is called by a church or placed in a church, whichever way it is done. He not only may be given an enormous amount of work—consider the illustration in the introduction—but also may make most of the decisions about the life of the church, sometimes in spite of his own reluctance. Why does this happen? Is it an unfortunate necessity because of the sad state of the church? Is it biblical?

One-man ministries abound for several reasons. First, we have a tradition that the job of the "minister" is to do all the ministry. "That's what he's paid for," the people may say, and they may want to keep it that way out of respect for tradition or through sheer laziness. Second, we have neglected the biblical emphasis on the body of Christ and the call to all church members to exercise their gifts in ministry. Third, sometimes there seem to be too few people in the flock who understand the truth well enough to help the pastor. Fourth, many people feel that they need theological training before they can take any responsibility in the life of a church. Fifth, some people just *like* to be in charge and have complete command of the church's ship. They are prepared to take on far too much work because, if they are seen taking so much responsibility, they are less likely to have their autocracy challenged. They unfortunately become builders and defenders of their own little kingdoms.

The clear New Testament pattern is to have several people joined in oversight of each local church. Paul wrote to Titus, "The reason I left you in Crete was that you might straighten out what was left unfinished and appoint elders in every town, as I directed you" (Tit 1:5; see also Acts 14:23; 20:17, 28; Phil 1:1). Not every elder was required to be a teacher or preacher, but it was required that each "hold firmly to the trustworthy message as it has been taught, so that he can encourage others by sound doctrine and refute those who oppose it" (Tit 1:9; see also Acts 20:28-31). Paul refers to the fact that *some* elders would be working at teaching and preaching (1 Tim 5:17), implying that this would not be true of all of them. All, however, were required to have a firm grasp of the truth so that each one could present and defend it. The New Testament also establishes the principle that those who devote themselves to teaching should be supported in some measure by the church, even though, like Paul, they might not claim their rights (1 Cor 9:12, 14; Gal 6:6; 1 Tim 5:17-18). Each church also had deacons (Phil 1:1; 1 Tim 3:8).

Paul himself worked with others whenever he could. He took men like Barnabas, Silas and Luke on his missionary journeys. He seems also to have worked alongside younger men, like Titus and Timothy, to train them in teaching and pastoring. Jesus too worked with a close circle of twelve and a wider one of seventy (Mt 10:1-10; Lk 10:1). Wherever we look in the New Testament, we find a shared ministry rather than a one-person work of teaching and oversight in the churches. Shared ministry is, of course, practically helpful, for it teaches mutual dependence and humility before each other and helps prevent a "this is my kingdom" mentality.

Training is important, as Paul makes clear to Timothy: "The things you have heard me say in the presence of many witnesses entrust to reliable men who will also be qualified to teach others" (2 Tim 2:2). However, we should not require all elders, whether teachers or not, to have formal theological training. The desire and commitment in all our churches should be to encourage those with gifts of teaching and leadership to develop and exercise their gifts.

On the most basic level, the *whole church* engages in ministry, not just elders and deacons. Paul writes that the calling of pastors and teachers is "to prepare God's people for works of service [ministry], so that the body of Christ may be built up until we all reach unity in the faith and in the knowledge of the Son of God and become mature, attaining to the whole measure of the fullness of Christ" (Eph 4:12-13). Elsewhere Paul says that God has given gifts to all his children and that we all ought to exercise our gifts in building up one another. We are all dependent on each other. Leadership and teaching are just two among many gifts (Rom 12:4-8; 1 Cor 12:1-31).

Some leaders may respond, "That is all very well in theory. But the sad reality is that people are not sufficiently trained, nor are they willing to be of help." As long as that is a pastor's attitude, nothing will change. We must take God at his word. He has gifted *all* his people, and they are quite capable of taking their part in many aspects of ministry if they are encouraged to do so. We need to have a vision for every member of the church taking his or her rightful place of service. And as God's Word is faithfully taught and lived, new leadership will continually emerge to be trained and brought into the oversight of the church.

4
AUTHORITY IN THE NEW TESTAMENT

*J*esus said to his followers, "If you hold to my teaching, you are really my disciples. Then you will know the truth, and the truth will set you free" (Jn 8:31-32). Jesus intended for us to find freedom in the truth, and the truth itself from his teachings. When the church functions as Paul describes it in Ephesians 4, the structures will encourage that process; members will be built up into maturity in truth and love, united with the church's head, Christ.

Then we will no longer be infants, tossed back and forth by the waves, and blown here and there by every wind of teaching and by the cunning and craftiness of men in their deceitful scheming. Instead, speaking the truth in love, we will in

all things grow up into him who is the Head, that is, Christ. From him the whole body, joined and held together by every supporting ligament, grows and builds itself up in love, as each part does its work. (Eph 4:14-16)
But the promise of life comes in adhering to the biblical teachings. Let us then look specifically at what the Word teaches about church leaders—apostles, elders and deacons—and learn from Scripture the proper roles of authority and discipline in the local church.

Apostles

Paul implies in 1 Corinthians 15:8 that he was the last of the apostles, "one born out of due time" (KJV). He says this because it was a requirement of apostleship to have been with Christ during his earthly ministry and to have been a witness of the resurrection of Christ.

After Judas had killed himself, Peter called the believers in Jerusalem to choose someone to take Judas's place among the apostles (Acts 1:17). The criteria Peter gives are two. First, "choose one of the men who have been with us the whole time the Lord Jesus went in and out among us, beginning from John's baptism to the time when Jesus was taken up from us." Second, "one of these must become a witness with us of his resurrection" (Acts 1:21-22). On these criteria Joseph Barsabbas and Matthias were put forward, and then God's choice was made known in the drawing of lots; Matthias took Judas's place (Acts 1:16).

So Paul calls himself an apostle "born out of due time" ("abnormally born," NIV); he had not been with Christ during his ministry. Only one of the criteria was true of Paul: he was a witness of the resurrection because Christ had made a special appearance to him on the Damascus road to appoint him as an apostle. "I have appeared to you to appoint you as a servant and as a witness of what you have seen of me and what I will show you. . . . I am sending [*apostellō*] you to open their eyes and turn them from darkness to light" (Acts 26:16-18; see also Acts 9:1-6; 22:6-15). Because Paul had not met the first criterion of being an apostle, he was always in the position of having to defend his apostleship.

So it was in both the church of Corinth and the church of Galatia. He had to remind church members that he was appointed directly by Christ; that his apostleship was not of a second order; that he was not a delegate appointed by other men, by other apostles, with no authority of his own from Christ. "I did not receive it [the gospel] from any man, nor was I taught it; rather, I received it by revelation from Jesus Christ" (Gal 1:11-12; see also vv. 15-17; 2 Cor 1:1; 12:12).

The question arises, Since Paul was born out of due time, could there not be *other* apostles since Paul's time also born out of due time? Paul seems to deny this possibility when he calls himself the last to whom Christ appeared: "And last of all he appeared to me also, as to one abnormally born" (1 Cor 15:8).

Even if someone today did claim to be a witness of the resurrection, in the sense that the New Testament apostles were eyewitnesses of the resurrection because Christ had appeared to them, there would still be problems. Who today could validate a claim to be appointed by Christ? Paul was in a unique position because the other apostles who had been with Christ during his ministry extended to Paul the right hand of fellowship and recognized his apostleship.

Paul says very carefully that his apostolic authority did not come from the other apostles, but that it came directly from Christ and through Christ. Yet at the same time Paul adds that the other apostles accepted his apostleship. "God, who was at work in the ministry of Peter as an apostle to the Jews, was also at work in my ministry as an apostle to the Gentiles. James, Peter and John, those reputed to be pillars, gave me and Barnabas the right hand of fellowship when they recognized the grace given to me" (Gal 2:8-9). Paul's extra apostleship was unique in that he lived at the same time as those who had been with Christ.

Consider, too, Peter's commendation of Paul's writings: "Bear in mind that our Lord's patience means salvation, just as our dear brother Paul also wrote you with the wisdom that God gave him. He writes the same way in all his letters, speaking in them of these matters. His letters contain some things that are hard to understand, which ignorant and unstable people distort, as they do the other Scriptures, to their own destruction" (2 Pet 3:15-16). Peter in this passage recognizes the authority of Paul. Nobody since that time can lay claim to the same kind of apostleship that was both claimed by Paul and recognized in him. New Testament apostleship is clearly unrepeatable, and consequently the authority accorded them belongs to no one since that time.

Unique Authority

The word *apostle* simply means "somebody sent out," a "missionary." But the implication of the word *apostle* in the New Testament and of the office of apostles is one of great authority, and therefore it is not helpful to use it today, even if one uses it in a secondary sense of "missionary" or "church planter."

The New Testament apostles had authority to teach new doctrine and to teach morals in a uniquely authoritative way. Consider Christ's promise to the apostles in John 16, where he says to them,

> I have much more to say to you, more than you can now bear. But when he, the Spirit of truth, comes, he will guide you into all truth. He will not speak on his own; he will speak only what he hears, and he will tell you what is yet to come. He will bring glory to me by taking from what is mine and making it known to you. All that belongs to the Father is mine. That is why I said the Spirit will take from what is mine and make it known to you. (Jn 16:12-15)

This promise was given to the apostles, as they were the ones with Jesus who could not bear to hear more just then, and it applies only to them. Jesus promised that he would give them the Holy Spirit, who would remind them of all he had said to them (Jn 14:26), who would bear witness to Christ along with them (Jn 15:26-27; Peter claimed this promise for the apostles in Acts 5:32), and who would teach them new things (Jn 16:13).

The apostles claimed that their teaching had the authority of Christ and of the Old Testament Scriptures. "If anybody thinks he is a prophet or spiritually gifted, let him acknowledge that what I am writing to you is the Lord's command" (1 Cor 14:37; 2 Thess 3:6, 14; 2 Pet 3:15-16, quoted above). If anybody today claims that the Spirit is teaching him new things, he is claiming an apostolic authority which is bound to cause trouble.

Several biblical passages, however, suggest that the term *apostle* might have been used in a wider sense than just the twelve plus Paul, but they are not conclusive. Romans 16:7 is one such passage. At first glance it looks as though Andronicus and Junias are numbered among the apostles. But the phrase "men of note among the apostles" (RSV) could mean that the apostles regarded Andronicus and Junias as noteworthy. Similar confusion applies to another passage, Acts 14:4 and 14, which can be construed to mean that Barnabas's ministry was regarded as apostolic because he was a coworker with Paul. Even here, though, it must be remembered that the Twelve and Paul were still alive to *recognize* Barnabas's ministry as apostolic.

Even if it were granted, however, that there is a wider use of the term *apostle* in the New Testament—in the sense of a church planter or a missionary like Barnabas—it would be very important to keep its dual usage clear and distinct. Barnabas may have been apostolic as a missionary and co-worker, but he is nowhere accorded the apostolic *authority* recognized in Peter and Paul, for example. If men today claim to be apostles, they must make quite clear that they are not by this designation claiming the authority of New Testament apostles like James and John. To make "apostle" an office in the church higher than elder or minister runs the danger of granting to the apostles an excessive authority, an authority rightly belonging only to men of the first century A.D. To whom are these modern apostles subject? Such apostles claim to submit to each other. But this is a problem if the group is small and contains one or two very dynamic men, which seems generally to be the case in such groups.

But let such modern apostles, for their own sakes and for the sake of the churches which they serve, set clear boundaries to their authority. Let them make plain that they are not apostles like Peter and Paul, nor are they in apostolic succession from Peter or Paul. Let them make plain that they do not have authority from God to teach anything new, and that all their teaching must be subjected to Scripture. Let them make plain that they have no authority from God to control the details of others' lives.

While our discussion has been about the use of the word *apostle,* it applies to any exaggeratedly authoritative leadership in the church. Some churches which do not use the title *apostle* nevertheless have leaders who claim or exercise unbiblical power and authority. It is not primarily the use of the word *apostle* which is at stake, but the attempted exercise of too much authority by whatever name it is called, be it archbishop, bishop, moderator, superintendent, leader or just Jim. Christ is the Christians' Lord, and no mediator is required between them. "I am in my Father, and you are in me, and I am in you" (Jn 14:20).

Elders and Deacons
As we examine the form of government in the New Testament church, we find there was a group of bishops or elders (the words are interchangeable in the New Testament) appointed in every church. Paul calls to him the elders of the church in Ephesus, but in his address to these elders he calls them bishops or overseers (Acts 20:17, 28). Acts 14:23 tells that Paul and Barnabas appointed elders in each church. 1 Timothy 3:1-7 gives the requirement for bishops. Titus 1:6-9 lists similar requirements for elders and then refers to these elders as bishops. In the same passage Paul requires Titus to "straighten out what was left unfinished and appoint elders in every town, as I directed you" (Tit 1:5).

Besides the elders, deacons were appointed to oversee practical matters and the administration of charity to the needy.

In those days when the number of disciples was increasing, the Grecian Jews among them complained against those of the Aramaic-speaking community because their widows were being overlooked in the daily distribution of food. So the Twelve gathered all the disciples together and said,

"It would not be right for us to neglect the ministry of the word of God in order to wait on tables. Brothers, choose seven men from among you who are known to be full of the Spirit and wisdom. We will turn this responsibility over to them and will give our attention to prayer and the ministry of the word."

This proposal pleased the whole group. They chose Stephen, a man full of faith and of the Holy Spirit; also Philip, Procorus, Nicanor, Timon, Parmenas, and Nicolas from Antioch, a convert to Judaism. They presented these men to the apostles, who prayed and laid their hands on them. (Acts 6:1-6; see also Rom 16:1; 1 Tim 3:8-13)

What authority did the elders in the New Testament church have? They were undershepherds of Christ. Peter writes of this in 1 Peter 5:1-3. "To the elders among you, I appeal as a fellow elder, a witness of Christ's sufferings and one who also will share in the glory to be revealed: Be shepherds of God's flock that is under your care, serving as overseers—not because you must, but because you are willing, as God wants you to be; not greedy for money, but eager to serve; not lording it over those entrusted to you, but being examples to the flock." Peter commands the elders not to lord it over those entrusted to them. Lording it over the flock means for elders to take the place of the Lord over his people, rather than being undershepherds of Christ responsible to teach and apply his Word.

The authority of elders in the New Testament is defined by the Word of God. Think of Paul's commandment to the elders of the Ephesian church: "I have not hesitated to proclaim to you the whole will of God. Keep watch over yourselves and all the flock of which the Holy Spirit has made you overseers. Be shepherds of the church of God, which he bought with his own blood. I know that after I leave, savage wolves will come in among you and will not spare the flock. Even from your own number men will arise and distort the truth in order to draw away disciples after them" (Acts 20: 27-30). The task of elders is to teach and guard the truth committed to them (see also 1 Tim 6:20; 2 Tim 2:2; 4:1-2). Paul in Titus 1:9 writes that elders are to instruct in sound doctrine and to refute those who contradict it.

James states strongly the responsibility of elders to teach only God's Word when he says that those who become teachers in the church must be very careful, because they will be judged more severely than others: "Not many of you should presume to be teachers, my brothers, because you know that we who teach will be judged more strictly" (Jas 3:1). That should warn all who are teachers or authorities in the church against extending their teaching, their authority, beyond the Word of God that has once been given. All who are in authority in the church will be judged by how they have taught and applied God's Word. They are not to teach and apply their own word, no matter how much they feel it is from God. Think of Paul's warning in 1 Corinthians 14:37-38, a passage which all in authority should apply to themselves: "If anybody thinks he is a prophet or spiritually gifted, let him acknowledge that what I am writing to you is the Lord's command. If he ignores this, he himself will be ignored." In other words, everybody must be subject to the authority of the New Testament apostles and their written word.

Discipline

In the New Testament we find that discipline was applied in two areas. In these situations Paul commanded that the authority of the elders be imposed on the congregation. The first was a case of serious doctrinal aberration, and the second involved serious moral misbehavior—disobedience to the commandments of God.

Paul writes of doctrinal error and discipline in 1 Timothy 1:19-20. "Some have rejected these [faith and a good conscience] and so have shipwrecked their faith. Among them are Hymenaeus and Alexander, whom I have handed over to Satan to be taught not to blaspheme."[1] From 2 Timothy 2:17-18 we learn that one of the errors of Hymenaeus was evidently to teach that the resurrection had already taken place.

John gives a doctrinal test for prophets to ascertain whether they have the Spirit of God or are false: Do they acknowledge that Jesus Christ has come in the flesh (1 Jn 4:1-3)? The churches in Revelation 2 are commended or rebuked on the basis of how they have dealt with false teaching (Rev 2:2, 15). Paul emphasizes in the strongest possible way the importance of preserving purity of doctrine in the church: "But even if we or an angel from heaven should preach a gospel other than the one we preached to you, let him be eternally condemned! As we have already said, so now I say again: If anybody is preaching to you a gospel other than what you accepted, let him be eternally condemned!" (Gal 1:8-9). Departure from the true gospel of Christ is clearly not to be tolerated; church discipline is the proper response to error.

Discipline for disobedience to the moral commandments of God's Word is just as clearly taught. In 1 Corinthians 5:1-5 discipline is administered in a case of incest. Other examples are refusal to work, sexual immorality, greed, idolatry, slander, drunkenness and swindling (1 Cor 5:9-11; 2 Thess 3:6, 10-15; Rev 2:14, 20). The New Testament describes with some care how this discipline ought to be carried out. First, we should go individually to the erring ones, to encourage them to accept their need for a change in their belief or behavior.

If they won't listen, then we should take one or two others along with us as witnesses. If they still won't listen, we should bring the matter before the church. Finally the church must take the very serious step of expelling them from the church (Mt 18:15-17; 1 Cor 5:1-11; and so on).

None of the situations calling for discipline in the Scriptures involved merely disagreement about a prophecy or a personal or practical matter; these do not call for discipline. When Paul and Barnabas disagreed over John Mark (Acts 15:36-39), they parted company, Paul taking Silas and Barnabas taking John Mark; but Paul did not discipline Barnabas. In fact, we find Paul later referring positively to Barnabas's ministry (1 Cor 9:6) and recognizing the value of John Mark's ministry also (Col 4:10; 2 Tim 4:12; Philem 24).

Consider also the different interpretation Paul puts on the prophecies given by Agabus and others concerning his coming imprisonment (Acts 21:10-14). That Paul disagrees with Luke and many others over whether to go to Jerusalem does not break up their fellowship, and certainly no one charges anyone else with rejecting God's authority or the prophet's. How different the New Testament handling of personal problems is from what happens in some twentieth-century churches! I have known a brother to be excommunicated for refusing to accept another's prophecy. I have known an "apostle" to be excommunicated for questioning a fellow apostle's application of discipline.

All the examples of discipline given in the New Testament arise either from disobedience to God's Word in the area of doctrine or from disobedience to God's moral commandments. Elders are given no authority to discipline beyond these two areas. There is no suggestion that elders should make the personal decisions of church members for them or that they have the right to make rules for the details of others' lives. Rather an elder's responsibility is to teach, exemplify and apply the Word of God. He is to be hospitable, to pray for and care for people, to serve, to counsel, encourage, reprove and rebuke, to rule and prophesy (Acts 20:28-31; 1 Tim 4: 11-16; 2 Tim 4:2; Tit 1:8-9; 2:1, 15; 1 Pet 5:1-3). In short, they are to be shepherds, shepherds whose authority is defined under the Word of Christ.

Authority Restricted

Just how specific *is* the teaching that God has given us in his Word? Even the apostles whom Christ had appointed, with their unique authority over the whole church, did not hand out decisions for the individual choices of people's lives. The teaching of the New Testament does not move beyond doctrine and the application of the moral law of God. It does not give rules or decisions for the specifics of people's lives: whom someone should marry, where people should live, what jobs they should hold, how much they should give to the church, whom they should go to for counsel. The apostles themselves restrict their authority to doctrine and moral obedience to God and do not extend it to the individual, specific details of people's lives. For example, we are told not to marry unbelievers (2 Cor 6:14), but to take a wife in a pure and honorable way (1 Thess 4:3-5); not to commit adultery (1 Cor 5: 9-10); not to fornicate or lust (Mt 5:27-28). But the choice *within those principles* of whom to marry is entirely individual. There is no suggestion that it must be covered by the church. God's way with us is a beautiful thing; he who made us knows our need for freedom. He has left us free to obey his law and to seek his face personally. We need not obey the supposedly superior spiritual authority of other people in nondoctrinal and nonmoral issues.

This is an important issue because often teachers in the church find themselves in positions of great respect. And if their teaching is sound, if the example of their lives is good, if individuals are becoming Christians through their ministry, then people tend to respect everything such teachers or elders say. Precisely because of this, those who are in a position of authority, rather than taking advantage of the respect that they hold, must be careful to restrict what they say to the application of God's Word. The elder must resist the temptation to tell other people what God's will for their lives is. Never should he become the Holy Spirit for anyone else.[2] No person in authority in the church has the right to think that he has superior insight into the will of God for other people, because in effect he then becomes the Lord to the other person; he becomes the Holy Spirit.

An elder or minister, of course, is responsible to counsel people, to offer advice and to warn about the possible consequences of decisions. But he must encourage people to make their own decisions before God and resist the temptation to make their choices for them, for doing so would imply that he knows God's will for their lives better than they do. In fear and trembling, trusting the Lord, the elder is to encourage people to go to the Lord themselves. The Lord has given them the freedom to make mistakes and to learn. What seems unwise to an elder may be the Holy Spirit's means of helping a person through difficulties and toward maturity. Human authority must never be added to the authority of God's Word and the Spirit in the person's own life; it must always be subordinate to the Word of God.

Whenever human authority oversteps these boundaries it produces bondage. It bears down with a crushing weight and cripples the spiritual life of believers. It results in immaturity in the church, growing inability among members to make decisions and increasing dependence on authority.

We must observe God's principles if we want freedom, the freedom of the Word. The freedom given by God's perfect law is the principle to remember. We ought not have the arrogance to suppose that we could ourselves develop structures more helpful for people than those the Word of God lays down. Even the appeal that such forms are only temporary, that they are for the stage of immaturity only, is invalid; for its claim is, in effect, that we know better than God's Word.

5

THE GIFT OF PROPHECY

What is the gift of prophecy and what authority does it have today? Before we answer this question from the New Testament's teaching on the subject, we will look at how prophecy is being used today and at some claims made for this gift.

Some people say that God makes his will for the believer's life known by speaking to the church through the prophetic gift. Sometimes a prophecy is given to the leaders, and at other times it has to be judged by them.

Behind this emphasis on prophecy lies a deep and honest yearning. People want to be open to God's new purposes for today; they do not want simply to copy the patterns and forms of the past. We need to question, however, whether the way prophecy is sometimes exercised and the weight it is accorded are, in fact, appropriate.

So, for example, one writer states: "The Holy Spirit's ministry of speaking to His church was not limited to the time of the twelve apostles. . . . To determine God's direction you need both the spoken and written word and both the Scriptures and the Holy Spirit speaking in the church."[1] In other words, in seeking God's direction, the individual Christian cannot be dependent simply on the Word of God and his own relationship with God through the Holy Spirit and Christ. He must go to the church for direction; that is, he must hear both God's written Word in the Bible and God's spoken word through his leaders. "Too long have we merely followed Christian principles or directives God spoke to his people in years gone by. . . . As believers we should *expect* to hear from God. The church responds by judging the word which is spoken, determining if it is true, and exhorting the people to obey what the Lord has said."[2] Again the individual has to submit to those in authority.

We can ask the question, How do these elders, ministers, pastors, bishops, know God's will not only for themselves but for others too? How do they know, when ordinary believers are unable to discern for themselves? The answer is that shepherds can go directly to God and ask for his will to be revealed, or they can go to the apostles (if they exist in the particular church) and ask them. This means in essence that the ordinary believer does not have sufficient access to God to discern his will, but has to submit to others his discernment of God's will.

This structuring of authority can lead to surprising results. In one local church Bruce, an elder, was suddenly commanded, on the strength of a prophetic utterance, to call one of his fellow elders "Father" and submit to him. In fact, the fellow elder was younger than he, only twenty-one. When Bruce refused to obey this command because he considered his fellow elder unfit for such authority, he was put out of the church for being rebellious. The consequences were tragic. It has taken Bruce and his wife several years to recover from this; it is not easy to be suddenly expelled from a group to which one has committed oneself. The adjustment for a committed Christian is particularly hard, since he has been told that he is disbelieving the Word of God spoken through the church leaders. It may be years before a person hurt in this way is ready to take an active part in any church.

Where leaders claim such authority over people's lives, demanding that everyone submit to them, the gift of prophecy has tremendous potential for misuse. This is particularly so if prophecy is understood as a word directly from the Lord. Elders, claiming they can say "Thus says the Lord" in the manner of the Old Testament prophets, can demand absolute obedience to their word.

A young man in another congregation was not prepared to accept the authority of the elders and bishops over his whole life. The church was deciding whether to put him out of fellowship. At this juncture came a prophecy, opening with these words: "I am the Lord God; listen to me now." That is a very serious thing to say. It asserts itself as absolute authority, the authority of God himself, the Creator and Redeemer, over someone else's life.

In another case a church leader told a congregation of eighty families, "The Lord says we are all to move to such and such a town." The town was hundreds of miles away. Everybody had to get up and go; otherwise they would have been told they were disobedient to God. There were doctors who had been serving in the community for many years and families with children in school, but everyone had to leave because this was "the word of God," not simply the word of a human leader. On this view, prophecy is given the same kind of authority over people's lives as Scripture itself.

You Claim You Can See
One leader wrote in a personal letter that he did not understand why the evangelical church emphasized so strongly the authority of Scripture when God speaks to us today through the gift of prophecy. This man understands "the word of God" or "the word of Christ" in such passages as Colossians 3:16 to refer to prophecy rather than Scripture.

With such views of the gift of prophecy, it is easy to move rapidly in new directions—not only practically but also doctrinally. There are no checks and balances in such a system. By its very nature it is open to abuse. What so often happens when a church understands prophecy this way is that it begins to have a higher and higher view of its own importance. It is the "spiritual" church, where others are "carnal." It is open to God's word for today, where others are not. It is the house of David, where others are the houses of Saul. It is God's remnant in an age of apostasy. The spirit of pride which may be engendered is alien to the spirit of humility which the Scripture commands us to preserve. "Blessed are the poor in spirit" (Mt 5:3). "Humble yourselves, therefore, under God's mighty hand" (1 Pet 5:6). "Now that you claim you can see, your guilt remains" (Jn 9:41). The end of the line is for such a church or group to start calling itself The Church.

Church history is littered with many sad examples of this. That this is a danger today is not just a figment of the imagination nor an attempt to be alarmist. It is already a reality in some groups.

The Local Church of Witness Lee is one such group. Lee is the central authority in the local churches: "When I command in my spirit, the Lord commands with me, for I am one spirit with the Lord." He rejects rational understanding of Scripture and demands a personal revelation, not just illumination, in the reading of Scripture. He teaches that Christ is the mingled God-man, and that in regeneration we too become mingled with God, becoming God-men. For Lee the church is Christ, and the believer must belong to its Local Church expression. Everyone must put off Christianity, which for him is every other denomination, "the wilderness," "Babylon," and flee to the Local Church.[3]

This is a sad conclusion for a church that began with a desire for the liberty of the Spirit, reacting against the license of the culture and the church, longing for commitment, longing for care, longing for a reality of life in the body of Christ. To ensure the reality of such body life, the Local Church developed structures which are not present in the Word of God. The consequence, however, is worse than the original problems which Lee and others were seeking to combat.

But is it in fact right to equate the gift of prophecy with "the word of the Lord"? Several examples have been cited which make this equation. The claim is that phrases like "the word of Christ," "the word," "the word of the Lord," common in many New Testament passages, refer not to the objective Christian message once for all given through Christ and his apostles, but rather to the gift of prophecy, a present-day revelation from Christ to the church. One writer expresses this in the following excerpts from an article entitled "The Prophet Today."

If someone claims that God has spoken fully and finally to us through the incarnation of his Son, we answer that his Son is still speaking (Ac 1:1), and that he does this by giving prophets to his church (Ep 4:11).

He is not merely a "Mouthpiece"; he has revelation and insight from God, and is commissioned to communicate, to act as God's spokesman, sharing out of a heart filled with vision and revelation.

The prophet is foundational (Ep 2:20), . . . and the church cannot be built without him. He brings revelation (Ep 3:4, 5), and sets direction.

Without the prophet, sects and denominations are born, relying on a fixed creed and formulated doctrines for their security, and utterly losing momentum and purpose in God.[4]

If this view is correct, then Paul's call to "let the word of Christ dwell in you richly" would be asking believers to give free rein to the gift of prophecy, free rein to direct words from Christ, rather than calling believers to meditate on the word of Christ found in Scripture itself.

Which of these views is correct?

The Word of God

In the New Testament we find a widespread use of the expression *the word of God*. Often it refers to the Old Testament, the written and authoritative Word (see Jn 10:35; 1 Tim 4:5). Against this background "the word of God" is then used to refer to God's revelation which proclaims Christ, the Word made flesh, and which is proclaimed by Christ (Jn 1:1, 14; 17:6-8, 14, 17; Tit 2:5; 1 Jn 1:10; 2:14). The living and written Word are not opposed but rather express a unity of spirit and message.

Because Jesus is the Word of God, and because the Word proclaims him, Jesus refers to the authority of his own word in the same way that he refers to the binding nature of the Old Testament word; for instance, "Whoever hears my word and believes him who sent me has eternal life" (Jn 5:24; see also Jn 8:31-32). "You have kept my word and have not denied my name" (Rev 3:8). Consequently, the apostolic writers use the expressions *the word of the Lord* or *the word of Christ* to speak of God's revelation in Jesus' teaching and life which centers on the message of his death and resurrection. This, to these specially appointed men, is the authoritative and final Christian truth (Acts 8:25; 12:24; 13:44; 19:10; 2 Thess 3:1; 1 Tim 6:3). As one lexicon puts it, the authoritative Christian message "is called simply ὁ λόγος = *the 'Word,'* since no misunderstanding would be possible among Christians"[5] (see Mt 13: 20-23; Acts 17:11; 18:5). The passage in Acts 17:11 expresses in the clearest possible way the unity between the new "word" and the Old Testament Scriptures: "These Jews . . . received the word with all eagerness, examining the scriptures daily to see if these things were so" (RSV).

Because of the authority of this word of Christ, the message about Christ spoken by the apostles is itself called the word of God; that is, it has the authority of Scripture (1 Thess 2:13; 2 Thess 2:15). This is true too of the written words of the apostles. And so the argument comes full circle, for the written New Testament is itself regarded as Scripture, the authoritative, written Word of God: "What I am writing to you is the Lord's command" (1 Cor 14:37; see also 1 Tim 5:18, where Paul quotes Deuteronomy and Luke equally as Scripture, and 2 Pet 3:2, 15-16). Gerhard Kittel writes quite properly that

the phrases "word of God," "word of the Lord" are very common in the NT, but . . . they are never used of special

divine directions. . . . The reason for this obvious and re-
markable fact is that after the coming of Jesus, the Word of
God or the Word of the Lord has for the whole of primitive Christianity a new and absolutely exclusive sense. It
has become the undisputed term for the one Word of God
which God has spoken, and speaks, in what has taken place
in Jesus and in the message concerning it. From this time
on, the term cannot be used of any other revealing event,
no matter how authentic and estimable. . . . The primitive
Christian conviction [is] that the revelation which has taken
place in Jesus Christ is definitive and unique.[6]

We must therefore conclude that there is no ground within
the New Testament for understanding the word of Christ to
refer to the gift of prophecy.

Prophecy
What, then, *is* the gift of prophecy, and what authority should
it have? In the New Testament the words *prophecy* and *prophet*
are used in several different contexts.

The most important usage refers to the Old Testament
prophets and their ministry. Examples of such reference
abound in the Gospels, where the narratives speak of the
prophets Jeremiah, Isaiah and so on (Mt 2:5, 17; 3:3; Lk 1:70;
4:17). Peter summarizes the attitude of Jesus and the apostles to the Old Testament prophets like this: "Above all, you
must understand that no prophecy of Scripture came about
by the prophet's own interpretation. For prophecy never had
its origin in the will of man, but men spoke from God as they
were carried along by the Holy Spirit" (2 Pet 1:20-21).

Jesus agreed completely with such a view when he spoke in
the Sermon on the Mount about the authority of the Old
Testament law and prophets: "Do not think that I have come

to abolish the Law or the Prophets; I have not come to abolish them but to fulfill them. I tell you the truth, until heaven and earth disappear, not the smallest letter, not the least stroke of a pen, will by any means disappear from the Law until everything is accomplished" (Mt 5:17-18). He confirmed again that the Old Testament prophets had spoken the word of God when he told the disciples on the road to Emmaus that they were foolish and slow of heart not to "believe all that the prophets have spoken" (Lk 24:25). Everything the Old Testament prophets prophesied had total, lasting and binding authority on the church of God. It therefore seems clear that Paul is referring to the Old Testament prophets in a passage like Ephesians 2:20, where he writes that the church is "built on the foundation of the apostles and prophets, with Christ Jesus himself as the chief cornerstone."

We should not use Ephesians 2:20 to try to give the New Testament gift of prophecy a binding authority in the church. The gift of prophecy exercised in the New Testament church was different from that special gift given to the Old Testament prophets. The latter were few in number, extending over a period of many centuries. Their word was binding when it was spoken and still is binding today. Their message, together with the writings of the authoritative New Testament apostles, is still the foundation of the church, for without their message written in Scripture we would have no Bible, no Word of God, no church. God gave them their gift for the whole church, from their day right up to the Second Coming of Christ.

In contrast, Paul writes to the church in the New Testament that *everyone* should desire the gift of prophecy and be eager to prophesy (1 Cor 14:1, 39). He defines prophecy as speaking for the "strengthening, encouragement and comfort" of the church (1 Cor 14:3). He clearly understands prophecy as speaking with the mind and contrasts it with speaking in tongues, which he calls speaking with the spirit (1 Cor 14: 13-17); the context of this statement is the discussion of tongues and prophecy in vv. 1-12). In other words, Paul does not understand the gift of prophecy as always and necessarily being a message given directly by the Holy Spirit—a "thus says the Lord" on every occasion. Rather he understands prophecy as a speaking with the mind for the practical up-building of the church, as a gift which all believers ought to be eager to exercise on behalf of one another.

I do not mean to imply that prophecy is simply a natural, human gift as opposed to some other supernatural, divine gift. The New Testament knows nothing of such a division between natural and supernatural, human and divine, ordinary and extraordinary. Paul and Peter see all gifts, whether teaching or prophecy, tongues or service, comforting or giving, healing or administering, interpreting or showing mercy, as gifts from God, given by the Holy Spirit for the benefit of the church, to be exercised in dependence on the Spirit and in love, with self-control, in a fitting and orderly way.

We have different gifts, according to the grace given us. If a man's gift is prophesying, let him use it in proportion to his faith. If it is serving, let him serve; if it is teaching, let him teach; if it is encouraging, let him encourage; if it is contributing to the needs of others, let him give generously; if it is leadership, let him govern diligently; if it is showing mercy, let him do it cheerfully. (Rom 12:6-8; see also 1 Cor 12:4-11, 28-31; 14:26-40; 1 Pet 4:10-11)

Thus Says the Lord?
Sometimes "thus says the Lord" can be spoken as if the prophet were putting the responsibility for what he says on God

rather than on himself. But this is wrong. The prophet must personally bear responsibility for what he or she says, and not hide behind any formula which suggests the prophecy is unquestionable because it comes directly from God with no human mediation.

If we could be certain that we were speaking the very words of God when we exercise the gift of prophecy, there would be no problem. But we can have no confidence of infallibility except where the Scripture speaks. Even though we are forgiven and have fellowship with the Spirit, we still make mistakes about what God is saying to us.

The claim to have authoritative words from God creates a problem because it contradicts what Scripture says about us and about our thoughts, words and deeds. "If we claim to be without sin, we deceive ourselves and the truth is not in us. ... If we claim we have not sinned, we make him out to be a liar and his word has no place in our lives" (1 Jn 1:8, 10). This apostolic principle applies to our discernment of God's will, to our exercise of prophecy and to our teaching, just as it does to every other area of our lives.

I am not suggesting that the gift of prophecy is inoperative in the church, but rather that we must recognize Christian fallibility. Sin may affect the functioning of any gift. Prophecy should be encouraged just as teaching is. But both these gifts should be exercised in humility, with a readiness to have one's words tested and judged, discussed and even rejected if they are found to be wanting.

We know from Acts that a prophecy may include a prediction of future events (Acts 20:23; 21:11), but we also know from Corinthians that this is not always the case. Whether a prophecy is a prediction or simply a practical word of wisdom to comfort someone who is discouraged, the prophecy is the responsibility of the person who speaks it; it does not come with absolute authority, as the words of the Old Testament prophets did.

Paul commands that prophecies be weighed and tested when they are given (1 Cor 14:29, 32), but he did not expect his own words to be weighed and tested this way. When he spoke as an apostle, he spoke with the authority of God himself—just as the Old Testament prophets had. But the non-apostolic gift of prophecy in the New Testament church did not have a binding authority on people's lives. Rather it was subject to the apostolic word, the Word of Scripture, the Word of God (compare 1 Jn 4:1-6).

Look again at the narrative beginning in Acts 20. In every town Paul visits, Christians prophesy that he will be imprisoned in Jerusalem (Acts 20:23; 21:11). Those who give the prophecies tell Paul he should not go to Jerusalem; they try to dissuade him (Acts 21:4, 12-14). Paul does not question the accuracy of the prediction. He even confirms it (Acts 20: 22-23; 21:13). He does not, however, regard the prophets' demands that he not go to Jerusalem as a command from the Spirit; he sees them as the people's human conclusion from what the Spirit had revealed. Instead he insists that the Holy Spirit is compelling him to go (Acts 20:22). Paul had to decide what he would do in light of what the Spirit had made known; these prophecies were only informative, not imperative.

We may draw some conclusions from this for us today. The gift of prophecy should be encouraged. It may include predictions about the future or particular messages from the Lord (Acts 13:1-2; 1 Tim 1:18; 4:14). Generally prophecy will be words of practical encouragement and comfort which all of us should seek to exercise in wisdom. Individuals must hold themselves responsible for their exercise of the gift of prophecy. Prophecy in the church is never a word of command from God, binding on its hearers, and it must not be used as such by either the elders or others anxious to get their way. When prophecies are given, even if predictions or specific messages are included, they must be weighed and tested; and the hearers are not bound to obey them. Rather, the hearers must seek the Lord's face to confirm for themselves what God's will is for their lives, just as Paul did when he decided to do the opposite of what the prophets suggested. Finally, only Scripture is binding. Prophecy today, just as any other teaching of the Word of God, is binding only when it is exposition of what Scripture clearly says.

I would appeal to those who regard prophecy as God's revelation for today to be aware of the dangers. Consider the examples of rapid drift away from biblical truth mentioned earlier in this chapter. Limit strictly the authority of your leaders. Re-examine your understanding of prophecy. Make sure you allow your Christian brothers and sisters the liberty of the Spirit.

6
NEW CHAINS FOR OLD

Where there is a hierarchical system for finding the will of God, covering for decision making or an authoritative word for the details of each other's lives from prophets, two difficulties emerge.

First, we lose the liberty of the Spirit; the individual is no longer free to seek the Lord for himself. In contrast, the New Testament teaches us that we grow to maturity as Christians by learning to find the will of God for ourselves and by being able to discern what is true and false, right and wrong, within the framework of clear teaching about truth and righteousness (Rom 12:1-2; Eph 4:11-16; Phil 3:15; 1 Thess 5:20-21; 1 Jn 2:20, 27; 5:13-15). Think too of Jesus' wonderful promise in Luke 11:9 and 13, "So I say to you: Ask and it will be given to you; seek and you will find; knock and the door will be opened to you. . . . If you then, though you are evil, know how to give good gifts to your children, how much more will your Father in heaven give the Holy Spirit to those who ask him!" Every believer, no matter how young in the faith, can be assured of the liberty of the Spirit and of help when wisdom is needed.

  Second, a new priesthood develops. A priest is someone who stands between the believer and God, taking requests for the believer to God, interceding on his or her behalf, then returning from the presence of God with the answer. This may seem an extreme way to describe the situation, but it is in fact accurate. If we say that the member must have important (or even not-so-important) decisions made by an elder, or if we say that the member must have such decisions covered or approved by a more mature Christian, we imply some or all of the following:

1. Because of immaturity most Christians are not able to bring their own requests for wisdom to God, but need someone else more mature to intercede on their behalf.

2. Because of immaturity most Christians are not able to discern the answer God gives, God's wisdom, and so need someone more mature to interpret God's will to them.

3. Because of immaturity most Christians cannot make their own ("uncovered") decisions.

4. Some Christians, either the more mature or the leaders, *are* mature enough both to make their own decisions and to approve or cover others' decisions.

  The clear implication of this is that the leaders have an access to God and an understanding of God's will denied to the ordinary member of the church. They have in effect become priests, mediators who stand between the believer and the Lord, for they have to pass judgment on an individual's understanding of God's will. Lost is the priesthood of all believers. A new priesthood of those in authority with the gift of prophecy takes its place. As Milton put it, "New Presbyter is but old Priest writ large."

The elders' calling is not to stand between the believer and God, but rather to lead the believer to stand before God. Elders should be teachers, ambassadors for Christ, undershepherds, servants, overseers—but not priests.

The Priesthood of All Believers

At the Reformation Martin Luther brought to light again a biblical doctrine which had become lost during the medieval period: the priesthood of all believers. John says in Revelation that Jesus "has freed us from our sins by his blood, and has made us to be a kingdom and priests to serve his God and Father" (Rev 1:5-6). Peter writes, "You are a chosen people, a royal priesthood, a holy nation" (1 Pet 2:9). All believers are priests.

What does it mean to be a priest? It means that every believer has direct access to God. Our priesthood is expressed when we pray for ourselves, seeking to obey God's Word and to find his will for our lives, and when we pray for and serve others, sacrificing our lives to the service of God.

Consider how Paul encourages us to bring our requests to God: "Do not be anxious about anything, but in everything, by prayer and petition, with thanksgiving, present your requests to God. And the peace of God, which transcends all understanding, will guard your hearts and your minds in Christ Jesus" (Phil 4:6-7). Does Paul say that a believer anxious about something should go to the elders and ask them? No, he urges the believer not to be anxious but to present his requests to God, because everyone is a priest through Christ.

Again, when the believer lacks wisdom, what do the apostles command? "If any of you lacks wisdom, he should ask God, who gives generously to all without finding fault and it will be given to him" (Jas 1:5). Of course, if a church is a living and caring church, people *will* discuss with one another, and with those they respect in the Lord, their problems and uncertainties about the decisions they are making. This is what it means for the church to be the body of Christ. The members of a church are to support and care for one another. We were not saved to be independent Christians, but Christians who are part of the church, a living, growing, interdependent body of people.

As priests we have the privilege of praying for ourselves through Christ our intermediary. But we have an equal responsibility to intercede on behalf of each other. Paul frequently asked people to pray for others and for himself. "And pray in the Spirit on all occasions with all kinds of prayers and requests. With this in mind, be alert and always keep on praying for all the saints. Pray also for me, that whenever I open my mouth, words may be given me so that I will fearlessly make known the mystery of the gospel, for which I am an ambassador in chains. Pray that I may declare it fearlessly, as I should" (Eph 6:18-20; see also Col 4:3-4; 1 Thess 5:25). We should go to others in our church and ask for their prayers when we face uncertainty about our future and when we need guidance, just as we do when we are sick.

We should be equally prepared to seek advice, comfort and encouragement from our fellow Christians. We are to "carry each other's burdens, and in this way . . . fulfill the law of Christ" (Gal 6:2). Part of the responsibility of a shepherd in the church is to help people work through difficulty and uncertainty. This responsibility, however, does not extend to telling somebody what God wants him to do, specifically, as if one knew this more clearly than the individual himself. In the end the shepherd's work must be to encourage the person to pray for the Spirit's leading and to make his own decision. The shepherd leads the sheep to the water—in this case, the Holy Spirit. The sheep must satisfy its own thirst. The Lord, the Shepherd of all, promises to satisfy the thirst of every one of his sheep by giving his Spirit and by giving wisdom, for he is a generous giver.

Our situation today is in striking contrast with the situation in the Old Testament. The people then were encouraged to go to the Temple, to the priest, and the priest used the Urim and Thummim and other means to find out God's will for people's lives. But now the veil which stood before the most holy place is torn down (Mt 27:51), and all believers with unveiled faces behold the glory of the Lord. "Whenever anyone turns to the Lord, the veil is taken away. Now the Lord is the Spirit, and where the Spirit of the Lord is, there is freedom. And we, who with unveiled faces all contemplate the Lord's glory, are being transformed into his likeness with everincreasing glory, which comes from the Lord, who is the Spirit" (2 Cor 3:16-18).

Conclusion

In conclusion, let us look back over the ground we have crossed. God, our infinite Creator, has given to us, his finite and sinful creatures, his law to direct our paths. The law of God lays down the structures for our lives and for the life of the church. God's structures are liberating for us, for as our Creator he knows us better than we know ourselves. In contrast, human structures, human forms, tend to bring bondage to our lives and to the life of the church when they exceed the law of God, even when the motivation behind them is good. Therefore, any structures we make for the church, whatever names we may give them, must be bounded by and limited to the forms given in the New Testament. To add to them, even in the name of bringing maturity and commitment, will in fact create immaturity and bondage in one form or another. Giving church leaders an authority which is more extensive than God's Word commands will cause problems.

In our day, society already produces many broken people who have difficulty making decisions, who naturally want to be dependent. If we try to help such people by encouraging a system of dependence, we simply make the problem worse. People already scarred by society or by their own past lives will become even more dependent, even less able to make decisions for themselves. Instead of being dependent upon the Holy Spirit, they will become dependent on human leadership.

But we have God's Word with its liberating forms, and we also have liberty in the Holy Spirit to approach God ourselves and ask for his direction for our lives. Christ's yoke was easy and his burden light in contrast to the heavy yoke and heavy burdens of the Pharisees who added to God's law. Today, too, Christ's yoke is easy and his burden is light compared to the heavy burdens of new authoritarian structures that people are tempted to impose within the church. As we obey the Spirit's structures, as we enjoy the Spirit's freedom, every one of us can begin to attain the glorious freedom of the children of God (see Mt 11:30; Rom 8:21).

APPENDIX: THE PLACE OF THE OLD TESTAMENT LAW

How much of the Old Testament law is applicable today? Many Christians, despite Jesus' strong words on the subject in Matthew 5:17-19, think that none of it applies. Others assume, somewhat arbitrarily, that only the Ten Commandments still apply, even though Scripture itself sees them as a statement of the central points of the law, rather in the way that "love the Lord your God" and "love your neighbor" are an encapsulation of all the commandments. In fact many of the Old Testament commandments are repeated in the Gospels and Epistles, so we should expect that much of the law would still be fulfilled in the Christian's life.

But the ceremonial law, including the sabbath law, has been fulfilled by Christ. "Therefore do not let anyone judge you by what you eat or drink, or with regard to a religious festival, a New Moon celebration or a Sabbath day. These are a shadow of the things that were to come; the reality, however, is found in Christ" (Col 2:16-17). "One man considers one day more sacred than another; another man considers every day alike. Each one should be fully convinced in his own mind. He who regards one day as special, does so to the Lord. He who eats meat, eats to the Lord, for he gives thanks to God; and he who abstains, does so to the Lord and gives thanks to God" (Rom 14:5-6). The priesthood and ceremonies were shadows or types of what Christ would do. "The next day John saw Jesus coming toward him and said, 'Look, the Lamb of God, who takes away the sin of the world!' " (Jn 1:29). "Get rid of the old yeast that you may be a new batch without yeast—as you really are. For Christ, our Passover lamb, has been sacrificed" (1 Cor 5:7; see also Heb 9:11-28; 10:1-18).

The ritual and dietary laws, which had once set Israel apart from other nations, have also been fulfilled, since the time of Israel's distinction as the nation of God has ended. Now Jewish and gentile believers are one people; the pilgrim church draws from all nations, so that these laws no longer apply to us. " 'Don't you see that nothing that enters a man from the outside can make him "unclean"? For it doesn't go into his heart but into his stomach, and then out of his body.' (In saying this, Jesus declared all foods 'clean.')" (Mk 7:18-19; see also Acts 10:9-15; Col 2:16). The many laws which made Israel and individual Israelites ritually clean, not only the food laws referred to in these passages, are no longer in effect.

I would suggest, too, that the laws prescribing certain punishments for doctrinal and moral disobedience also functioned primarily to keep Israel's distinctive calling as a nation; as the people of God, Israel was to be an example to surrounding countries of the awful seriousness of disregarding

God's Word and law. In the New Testament, doctrinal or moral disobedience is to be punished by church discipline and excommunication
rather than by the sword which removes a false prophet, an idolater or an
adulterer bodily from the state. "It is actually reported that there is sexual
immorality among you, and of a kind that does not occur even among
pagans: A man has his father's wife.... When you are assembled in the
name of our Lord Jesus and I am with you in spirit, and the power of our
Lord Jesus is present, hand this man over to Satan, so that the sinful nature
may be destroyed and his spirit saved on the day of the Lord" (1 Cor 5:1,
4-5; see also Rev 2:2, 14-15, 20).

What then remains of the law for today? The moral laws apply to the life
of the individual and describe the character of one who desires to reflect the
image of God. "You were taught, with regard to your former way of life, to
put off your old self, which is being corrupted by its deceitful desires; to be
made new in the attitude of your minds; and to put on the new self, created
to be like God in true righteousness and holiness" (Eph 4:22-24; see also
Lev 19; Col 3:5-10).

Many laws for Israel as a state cannot be applied to us directly for two
reasons. First, our callings are different. Israel was called to be God's nation
in a particular geographical location, while the church has been called to
scatter over all the earth, like salt. Second, the circumstances in our mo-
ments of history are different.

The laws for the state of Israel, however, certainly contain many principles we should seek to see embodied in the laws of our country: laws about
justice in judgment and against partiality and corruption; laws about integrity and fairness between employers and workers; laws about fair pricing;
laws about the care of the poor, the widow, the orphan and others in
desperate need; laws requiring that each new generation be given the possibility of a new beginning, despite the failures or misfortune of the previous
generation (see the sabbath and Jubilee Year laws). We should still be con-
cerned about those areas which were of concern to God, where infringe-
ments were heavily punished in Old Testament times, because they involved matters fundamental to *any* healthy state; for example, the value of
human life, born and unborn, the sanctity of family life and sexuality. And
we should acknowledge too the necessity of punishing evildoers. God has
always viewed people as responsible for their actions; crime is not purely
environmentally caused.

We as Christians ought to examine carefully the Old Testament law to
discover other areas where principles could suggest political and social
change appropriate for our day. Our culture is in confusion and has no
sound basis for social, political and moral improvement. God's law gives

us that basis, and we fail to be the salt of the earth if we abandon our society to wander along its present directionless path, or if we simply copy the empty clichés of one or another party and sprinkle them with a little Christian holy water.

Finally, in one sense the whole of the Old Testament law applies to us today and is to be fulfilled in our lives. Paul applies the language of the ceremonial and sacrificial laws to the Christian life. Instead of presenting animals, we are to present *ourselves* as living sacrifices. "Therefore, I urge you, brothers, in view of God's mercy, to offer your bodies as living sacrifices, holy and pleasing to God—which is your spiritual worship. Do not conform any longer to the pattern of this world, but be transformed by the renewing of your mind. Then you will be able to test and approve what God's will is—his good, pleasing and perfect will" (Rom 12:1-2; see also 1 Cor 3:17; 5:8; 6:19; 2 Tim 4:6; 1 Pet 2:5). The ritual laws were outward signs of a heart and life set apart, a holiness of life to which believers today are also called (Mt 15:1-20).

The Old Testament punishment of death for false teaching stands as a warning to us of the dreadful seriousness of leading people astray. Those who teach are awesomely responsible to be true to God's message (Gal 1:8; Jas 3:1). We must keep our doctrine pure (1 Tim 4:16).

We should also be warned by the Old Testament's serious punishments for moral offenses, which Paul underlines so firmly: "Do you not know that the wicked will not inherit the kingdom of God? Do not be deceived: Neither the sexually immoral nor idolaters nor adulterers nor male prostitutes nor homosexual offenders nor thieves nor the greedy nor drunkards nor slanderers nor swindlers will inherit the kingdom of God" (1 Cor 6:9-10; see also Eph 5:5-6). The New Testament reaffirms the Old Testament's call to holiness of life.

Let us not then disregard or pour contempt on the Old Testament law; it too is part of that law of liberty which is more precious than fine gold.

NOTES

Chapter 2: The Word and the Spirit

[1]Neil T. Duddy and the SCP, *The God-Men: An Inquiry into Witness Lee and the Local Church* (Downers Grove, Ill.: InterVarsity Press, 1981), p. 41.

[2]Arthur Jones, *All the Fulness of God*, booklet no. 1, *The Law of the New Life* (Mussoorie, U.P.: Seemant Prahari Press, n.d.), p. 36.

[3]Ibid., pp. 44, 46.

[4]Watchman Nee, *The Release of the Spirit* (Witney, Oxon: Sure Foundation Publishers, 1965), p. 89; and *The Spiritual Man*, 3 vols. (New York: Christian Fellowship Publishers, 1968), 1:149, 151.

[5]Nee, *Release of the Spirit*, pp. 92-94; *Spiritual Man*, pp. 80, 93, 150, 186; *The Normal Christian Life* (London and Eastbourne: Victory Press, 1957), p. 111.

[6]These laws were designed to set Israel apart from other nations before the coming of Christ. They included, for instance, circumcision, dietary laws and festival observance. Cf. Gal 6:12-16; Col 2:16-17.

[7]F. F. Bruce, *Commentary on the Epistles to the Ephesians and the Colossians* (Grand Rapids: Eerdmans, 1957), p. 283.

[8]John Calvin, *Commentary on the Gospel according to St. John*, 2 vols. (Grand Rapids: Eerdmans, 1956), 2:145-46. See also Calvin *Institutes* 1. 9. 1-3.

Chapter 3: Some Danger Areas

[1]Jack Sparks and Arnold Bernstein, "A Letter from the Elders to the People of the Church Which Includes CWLF," 16 July 1975.

[2]Jack Sparks, "The Apostolic College," paper distributed to EOC elders, pp. 1, 26.

[3]Watchman Nee, *The Body of Christ: A Reality* (New York: Christian Fellowship Publishers, 1978), p. 48.

[4]Ibid., p. 20.

[5]Ibid., pp. 21-22, 54.

[6]Ibid., p. 68.

[7]Ibid., p. 69.

[8]Ibid., p. 74.

[9]Ibid., pp. 74, 76.

Chapter 4: Authority in the New Testament
[1]See also 1 Cor 5:5.
[2]Francis Schaeffer has given this excellent advice in personal conversation on many occasions.

Chapter 5: The Gift of Prophecy
[1]Dick Ballew, *The Place Where God Lives* (Mt. Hermon, Calif.: Conciliar Press, n.d.), p. 8.
[2]Peter E. Gillquist, *Fresh New Insight into Love Is Now*, p. 122.
[3]Witness Lee, *Romans, Recovery Version* (Anaheim, Calif.: Living Stream Ministry, 1974), p. 26. See also *The God-Men*.
[4]John MacLauchlan, "The Prophet Today," *Proclaim!* no. 1, March 1981, pp. 1-4.
[5]Walter Bauer, "λόγος," *A Greek-English Lexicon of the New Testament and Other Early Christian Literature,* trans. and ed. William F. Arndt and F. Wilbur Gingrich (Chicago: University of Chicago Press, 1957), p. 479.
[6]Gerhard Kittel, "λέγω," in *Theological Dictionary of the New Testament,* ed. Gerhard Kittel and Gerhard Friedrich, trans. Geoffrey W. Bromiley, 10 vols. (Grand Rapids: Eerdmans, 1964-76), 4:113.